PILGRIMS

The Archbishop of Canterbury's Lent Book

PILGRIMS

Stephen Platten

Foreword by
the Archbishop of Canterbury

Fount
An Imprint of HarperCollinsPublishers

For Rosslie, Aidan and Gregory

– fellow pilgrims

Fount Paperbacks is an Imprint of
HarperCollins*Religious*
Part of HarperCollins*Publishers*
77–85 Fulham Palace Road, London W6 8JB

First published in Great Britain
in 1996 by Fount Paperbacks

1 3 5 7 9 10 8 6 4 2

© 1996 Stephen Platten

Stephen Platten asserts the moral right to be
identified as the author of this work

A catalogue record for this book is
available from the British Library

ISBN 0 00 627954 6

Printed and bound in Great Britain by
Caledonian International Book Manufacturing Ltd, Glasgow

CONTENTS

FOREWORD

Travelling overseas with Stephen Platten is an unforgettable experience. During my first four years as Archbishop, when he was serving as my Secretary for Ecumenical Affairs, those journeys took us to countries as disparate and different as Israel and Italy; Russia and Romania; Greece and Georgia; America and Armenia. Sometimes we travelled in comfort and style, sometimes only with great difficulty, but Stephen was always present with his fund of anecdotes and infectious laugh, coupled with his encyclopaedic knowledge of our great sister churches and the subtleties of ecumenical sensitivities and debates.

Travelling with him also revealed other sides of Stephen's character. He is a man of prayer who, as a Franciscan tertiary, takes the discipline of Christian spirituality very seriously. He is also a man of vision who is always on the look-out to do new things in new ways. Both these he links to his deep sense of the history of the places he visits. To think of Stephen, then, is to think of pioneers like Columba, Paulinus, Aidan and Augustine and the abbeys and islands associated with them.

Given this background it was, therefore, no surprise that he became so closely linked with the celebrations marking the fourteen hundredth anniversaries of the arrival of St Augustine as the first Archbishop of Canterbury and of the death of St Columba. 'Pilgrims' Way', as those celebrations have come to be known, will see pilgrims from England, Wales, Scotland and Ireland, together with others from Italy and France, travelling to and worshipping in those places forever associated with those two great saints and the traditions of which they are symbols.

It was for those reasons that I invited Stephen to write this, my 1997 Lent Book, focusing both on them and on the theme of pilgrimage. What has resulted in the pages that follow is a book with many facets. From one angle it is, as Stephen says, a short handbook to some of the major holy places linked to the early years of Christianity in the British Isles. From another it is a historical study providing an overview of the key characters and events that shaped the Christian mission in this country. From yet another it is a theological study, bringing together as it does his reflections on the Roman and Celtic understandings of Church life and of spirituality. In doing so he describes their differences but also the enormous amount that they have in common. Finally it is also a devotional book, challenging us all to a deeper commitment to Christ in our everyday lives. It is not just a description of pilgrimage, but rather a handbook for pilgrims – pilgrims who want to get in touch with some of the roots of their faith and then to live that faith in the present.

This is a book to dip into, as well as one to read all at one go. It is a book to keep on your shelves and to turn to, not just in 1997, but for many years to come. I warmly commend it.

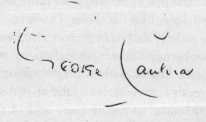

George Cantuar

INTRODUCTION

The opportunity to reflect upon the significance of Augustine of Canterbury and Columba in precisely this way comes but once every hundred years. It would be easy to view it simply in historical terms. The fact, however, that Christianity in Britain and Ireland owes its origins to the dual roots of the Celtic and Roman missions has more to offer us than the purely historical. For in these two traditions there are contrasts and complementary elements from which we can still learn so much.

During the fourteenth centenary year, pilgrimages will cross Europe and the islands of Ireland and Britain. Often the pilgrims will celebrate at the ancient sites associated with the early missionaries, but they will also travel through the great cities of our lands. They will thus encounter industrial and urban landscapes as well as the remoter parts of the countryside. The chapters which follow are intended to stimulate reflection upon the implications of these roots of Christian mission for contemporary life.

The book is called *Pilgrims* both to connect with the celebrations which will take place and to emphasize the fact that Christian life itself, for individuals and communities, is a pilgrimage. For that reason too, each chapter begins in a particular place and with a particular individual or individuals. To visit the sites associated with the Christian missions of the seventh and eighth centuries is to encounter again the people who brought the gospel here and to feel something of the motivation behind each life and pilgrimage. In that sense, this book may also act as something of a handbook for those who, in the coming years, may seek to visit these holy places. It does not pretend to be either a tourist guidebook or an exhaustive theology. Instead, alongside its main task, it aims to introduce these sites and to offer also an introduction to some of the theological and spiritual themes evoked by an encounter with those holy places and holy people. These themes are as challenging and important to humanity in the twentieth and twenty-first centuries as they were in the year 597.

There are so many people to whom I owe gratitude in preparing this book. First and foremost I am grateful to the Archbishop of Canterbury for inviting me to write the book. Then I would particularly mention Sister Renate, CHN, and Canon Andrew Deuchar who read the manuscript material and were always helpful in their reflections and criticism. Brother Harold Palmer of Shepherd's Law was most helpful as I sought to work out the original plan of the book. My thanks to those who typed the manuscript – Jean Mitchison and Fiona Millican at Lambeth, and Margaret Smith in Norwich. Finally, I should thank Rosslie, my wife, not only for reading chapters and commenting helpfully but also in putting up with the endless hours of writing – even as we moved house.

Deo gratias

Stephen Platten
Norwich Cathedral
Advent 1995

USING THE BOOK IN GROUPS

Those using the book in study groups may wish to take the chapters two at a time per week, working through from the beginning. However, it may well be more profitable to use two at a time, one from each section, thus using the historical and the applied each week, i.e. 1 and 6, 2 and 7, etc. Questions designed to stimulate discussion based on the principal themes of the book can be found on page 208.

SELECTIVE CHRONOLOGY

c. 209   Martyrdom of St Alban

325   Council of Nicaea

c. 375   Anglo-Saxon settlements begun in Britain

c. 398   St Patrick born probably in Britain or Gaul

397   Death of St Ambrose in Milan and St Martin of Tours. St Ninian builds his church at Whithorn

c. 480   Birth of St Benedict in Nursia in Umbria

c. 500   Celtic monasteries established in Cornwall

c. 521   St Columba born at Garton, Donegal

c. 544   Foundation of the monastery at Clonmacnoise by St Ciaran

c. 560   Dewi (St David) founds the cathedral at St Davids

596   Pope Gregory the Great sends Augustine to lead mission to Britain

597   St Augustine arrives at Ebbsfleet and establishes a monastic church in Canterbury. Columba dies on Iona

603   Death of St Mungo (Kentigern) at Glasgow

604   Dioceses established in Rochester and London

618   St Kevin dies at Glendalough

627   St Paulinus baptizes King Edwin

633   St Felix founds a church in Felixstowe; the beginnings of a church in East Anglia

c. 635   St Aidan preaches in Northumberland

654   St Cedd begins a church at Bradwell. Wilfrid travels to Rome with Benedict Biscop

664   St Cuthbert arrives in Lindisfarne; the Synod of Whitby

668   St Theodore of Tarsus Archbishop of Canterbury

675   St Hilda and Caedmon at Whitby; St Etheldreda at Ely

731   Bede completes his *Ecclesiastical History of the English People*

775   Martyrdom of St Boniface in Frisia

Iona •

• Glasgow

Lindisfarne •

Hexham • Jarrow •
Durham •

Whithorn •

Whitby •

Ripon •

Ceanannus
Mor (Kells) •

• Clonmacnoise
Kildare •
Glendalough •

Lincoln •

Lichfield •

Ely •

St Davids •

St Albans •

Bradwell •

Ebbsfleet •

Canterbury •

Perranporth •

A DOUBLE
INHERITANCE

ONE

PILGRIMAGE

We explore the origins and development of pilgrimage both as a discipline within Christian spirituality and as an image for the Christian life.

SAINTS, SHRINES AND PILGRIMS

It is the just man who
Like a bold lion, should be without fear.
I am here.
No traitor to the King. I am a priest,
A Christian, saved by the blood of Christ,
Ready to suffer with my blood.

So speaks Thomas à Becket in T. S. Eliot's *Murder in the Cathedral*. These rousing, heroic words reflect only one part of the subtle weave of Eliot's poetic play. For Becket was a saintly exemplar, a holy and courageous divine slain by the hand of a tyrant, but he was also a stubborn and unrealistic prelate devoid of political sense. The King's anger towards him remains culpable but understandable in the circumstances. Becket is an ambiguous saint. In seeking to protect ecclesiastical courts as separate from those of the state, he could be accused of pleading on behalf of a compromised clerical caste who deserved punishment alongside the rest of the criminal populace.

Despite this ambiguity, however, it was his bloody martyrdom at the hands of the King's men that lent to Thomas à Becket the halo of a saint. Through his canonization and the growth of his cult, Canterbury was firmly established as a centre for pilgrimage.

Canterbury was already a significant centre. It had been occupied before the Romans established it as the city of Durovernum and it later became the seat of a Kentish King. So it was when Augustine arrived from Rome in 597 to convert the native population, including the court of King Ethelbert, and to establish Canterbury as the first bishopric of his Roman mission. Each of these factors gave to Canterbury an eminence which placed it above other cities. Becket's murder, however, transformed Canterbury into one of the two primary centres of pilgrimage in medieval England, alongside the shrine of Our Lady at Walsingham. Until this time, it had been Cuthbert, the seventh-century Celtic Abbot and Bishop of Lindisfarne, who had been England's most revered saint.

Canterbury's dramatic transformation into a great centre of pilgrimage is clear from contemporary historical evidence. Martyred on 29 December 1170, Becket was canonized in the following February. The normal complex rigmarole of saint-making had been short-circuited. Doubtless the rapid growth of a cult around Becket was the cause of this swift sanctification. The growth of the cult is clear from other evidence too. Churches were dedicated to his memory very soon after his martyrdom. We might expect that some nearby churches would have received such dedication; the remarkable Church of St Thomas à Becket, Fairfield in Romney Marsh, now standing in splendid rural isolation and often cut off by flood waters, is one such local dedication. But the cult spread both swiftly and broadly. What is now the Cathedral Church of St Thomas of Canterbury in Portsmouth received its dedication when French monks from Normandy established the foundation *c.* 1185, only fifteen years after Thomas's death.

Becket's martyrdom left its mark on the wider political scene. St Laurence O'Toole, who acted as peacemaker between Strongbow and the English invaders when Dublin was overrun in 1170, visited Henry II. He negotiated a treaty between the King and Rory O'Connor, the High King of Ireland, in 1172. During that same visit, O'Toole made a pilgrimage to Becket's shrine at Canterbury and himself just escaped martyrdom at the hands of a lunatic assassin. After King Henry II himself made a penitent pilgrimage to Becket's shrine, a pilgrims' route for people from all over medieval Europe was soon established. Europe, as we shall see later, was not as paralysed by the slowness of journeys over vast distances in medieval times, as some have led us to believe. Britain was arguably less insular and isolated from mainland Europe then than psychologically it often appears to be in the present day.

Canterbury's significance as a pilgrim centre is still apparent today. 'Pilgrims' Way' over the North Downs remains a well-known and well-trodden path. 'Pilgrims' Rest' and 'Pilgrims' Hotel' remain popular names for hostelries, guest houses and restaurants both within Canterbury and along the roads that lead to the great shrine. The medieval cathedral, with the stately magnificence of the great central Bell Harry tower and the soaring heights of the perpendicular nave, is as fitting a focus for the modern pilgrim as it was for the pious traveller of the late Middle Ages. Canterbury itself as a city, and pilgrimage as a spiritual exercise, have been immortalized for the English-speaking world through the writings of Geoffrey Chaucer. Written in Middle English, Chaucer's work represents one of the crowning achievements of medieval English literature and it is structured entirely around the journey tales of Canterbury pilgrims.

ROOTS OF PILGRIMAGE

Pilgrimage has become a popular and sometimes almost commonplace theme in contemporary Christianity. It is easily hijacked by bogus forms of Romantic idealism which are themselves taken over by the commercialism of a materialistic age. Chaucer mugs vie with Becket T-shirts, luring people to empty their wallets into the coffers of the cunningly designed souvenir centres and gift shops. The story of the growth of Becket's cult and of the power of pilgrimage, however, serve to teach us a broader lesson. The medieval pilgrims identified the courage of Becket (despite the other ambiguities of his character) with the gospel of Christ. That gospel was rooted in self-giving love and culminated in the cross and resurrection.

These powerful images resonated with the consciousness of popular piety. Relics of holy martyrs held a power all of their own; the prayers of the saints had an intrinsic efficacy. The holiness of such places rubbed off on the 'common man'. Healing, penitence and simple growth in holiness were just some of the expectations of medieval pilgrims. Not all of these expectations have survived in every contemporary Christian tradition. The essential message of pilgrimage itself, however, has a very long history and its central focus remains common to an enormous variety of different traditions. It retains its power, a power which has been rediscovered again and again in the present day.

The roots of pilgrimage can be traced back to the story of Abraham in the Old Testament (Genesis 12:1 ff.). Abraham sets out with his family into a strange land, following the call of God. Abraham responds to God's promise that his people will be taken into a new land where they will both be blessed and be a blessing to others. But it would be a narrow view that restricted pilgrimage to the Judaeo-Christian tradition. The pagan deities of antiquity had their own cultic centres and shrines. The most famous shrine of ancient Greece, which still retains something of its identity, is that of Apollo at Delphi. The powerful attraction of a holy place remains palpable in the atmosphere there. Pilgrims would approach Delphi on particular days to celebrate a specific festival of Apollo. Such was also the case with the Temple in Jerusalem.

Elsewhere beyond the Judaeo-Christian tradition are other patterns of spirituality which include some parallels with pilgrimage. Aboriginal communities in Australia within their spiritual patterns of dreaming include the so-called 'Songlines', music through which the individual and the community may sing their journey through life. As Bruce Chatwin writes,

> each Ancestor, while travelling through the country, was thought to have scattered a trail of words and musical notes along the line of his footprints ... A song was both map and direction finder. Providing you knew the song, you could always find your way across country ... I felt the Songlines were not necessarily an Australian phenomenon, but universal ...'

There appears to be a human instinct which combines religious sensitivity with travelling out from one's home. The music or story-telling owes its character and significance to the journey. Already we have seen this to be a feature of the Judaeo-Christian scriptures in the Old Testament. It is there in the New Testament too.

In Hebrews 11:13, in some translations of the Greek, the image of pilgrimage is used to describe the Christian life itself: 'These all died in faith, not having received what was promised, but having seen it and greeted it from afar, and having acknowledged that they were strangers and pilgrims on the earth'. More recent translations prefer to talk of strangers and exiles, sojourners or aliens. Despite the slightly different nuance, later views of pilgrimage also often retain this sense that we are aliens or sojourners in a strange land, preparing for our arrival in the nearer presence of God.

More central still to the Christian life and Christian theological expression is the gospel tradition itself. The four gospels are often described as 'Passion narratives with extended introductions'. The accounts of the Passion are believed to be the most ancient continuous narrative elements within the gospels. The material preceding the Passion narratives and describing Jesus' ministry was already in existence before the gospels reached their present form, but was knitted together later. Many scholars now believe that the Passion narratives reached their present form and structure as a result of being at the centre of pilgrimage liturgies. The story of Jesus' Passion, death and resurrection was acted out in procession moving between the holy places within Jerusalem, culminating at Calvary and then at the site of the empty tomb. The modern pageants and dramas which re-enact 'The Way of the Cross' in the streets of our cities, which are themselves a form of pilgrimage, may reflect customs which take us back to the heart of the gospels from the earliest days of the Christian Church.

Although there may remain conjecture about the Passion narratives as pilgrimage liturgies, there is no doubt about the existence of such patterns of pilgrimage in Jerusalem from the fourth century onwards. *The Pilgrimage of Egeria* (Etheria) tells the story of the journey of a Spanish Abbess to the Levant at the end of the fourth century. Old Testament locations are mentioned, but then sites from the Passion of Jesus are pinpointed and related to the patterns of daily prayer of the Church. It may even be that some of the traditions which associate certain holy sites with particular places in the Old City of Jerusalem, and give direction and orientation to the Via Dolorosa, date back to this early pattern of pilgrimage. Contemporary tours in Jerusalem and the Holy Land strike similar notes and often contain a mixture of the educational and the liturgical, the didactic and the pious. As it has come down to us in the present day, much of the pilgrimage tradition is the fruit of medieval development. It is the world of Chaucer that is often most vividly recaptured in the popular imagination. But we can see that within medieval times, and in antiquity, Christian pilgrimage was not simply the invention of our ancestors in these islands.

WHY JOURNEY?

In the early Christian Church the tradition was firmly biblical. In particular, there were two reasons for pilgrimage. The first was to follow the pattern of Abraham, to wander for God, having but a tent for one's home and moving always onward. The second was the penitential pilgrimage, as in the case of King Henry II. Often pilgrims were required to assume the role of a wayfarer begging for their livelihood and working out their salvation on the road. This idea that walking dissolved crimes of violence was linked with the wanderings forced upon Cain to atone for the murder of his brother.

Clear traces of the biblical roots of pilgrimage and of further developments in the early Church are also visible in what we know of the Celtic understanding of pilgrimage. For Irish Christianity there was also a strong connection between martyrdom and pilgrimage. Pilgrimage was a particular form of martyrdom; the individual's own will was resigned to the will of God. The self-giving love of Christ already alluded to, is reflected in the extreme self-denying instincts of the single-minded search for God on this earth. For some, this meant the pilgrimage of Abraham, but perhaps pursued with even less clarity about the nature of the destination or the precise means by which God's promise to all humanity would be fulfilled. The *Anglo-Saxon Chronicle* describes the impractical plans of three Irishmen in 891:

> And three ... came to King Alfred in a boat without any oars from Ireland, which they had left secretly, because they wished for the love of God to be in foreign lands, they cared not where. The boat in which they travelled was made of two and a half hides, and they took with them enough food for seven days. And after seven days they came to land in Cornwall ...[2]

The pattern of the wanderer, seemingly aimless in regard to geographical destination, is repeated; it is an exaggerated variation on the theme of Abraham.

Some pilgrims believed there to be an idyllic island, similar to the land of milk and honey, where the rule of Christ's kingdom was already established. Often the pattern of St Anthony, in the Egyptian desert, was mirrored. Here the pilgrimage was that of a hermit or anchorite. The journey for God this time was not geographical in its trajectory but instead an inner pilgrimage. Sites for such a hermit's life were plentiful around these islands. One of the most dramatic is that of Skellig Michael, a jagged, rocky island, seven miles off the coast of Ireland, where the remains of a small oratory are still visible. In Wales, the monastic roots and tradition of pilgrimage to Bardsey Island, off the Lleyn peninsular, go back centuries. The Celtic mission to Northumbria spawned cells both on the mainland as for example at Warkworth and again also out to sea. Lindisfarne, the Farne Islands off Bamburgh, and Coquet Island, just off the coast near Amble at the mouth of the River Coquet, are just some examples.

Not only was pilgrimage associated with a life of self-denial, solitude and contemplation, it was also often combined with a missionary vocation. Here, however, the understanding of the nature of mission and the character of a missionary's life would vary fairly sharply. It could certainly mean that monks and holy men would make pilgrimage far from their original homes, reaching out into tracts of heathen countryside. The establishment of the minster churches and their model of mission is testimony to this. But this is to anticipate later chapters. Missionary work for many of these early Celtic pilgrims meant a life of contemplation and self-denial; it was equivalent to the life of the hermit. There might be no deliberate policy to go out into the surrounding countryside in search of converts.

In all this, however, the sense of place and journeying remained paramount, even if ultimately it promised a life of total solitude in the same place for the rest of the monk's life. The Celtic tradition was sensitive to the world, to nature and to place. The ancient Celtic sites at Glendalough, south-west of Dublin, or Iona in the Hebrides, at Penmon on Anglesey and at Lindisfarne remain evocative places. They breathe the air of places where holy men and women have trodden their earthly pilgrimage and lived holy lives.

DEVELOPING PATTERNS

In the medieval period, pilgrimage saw its full flowering. The great pilgrim routes have left clear marks upon the countryside through which they made their way. Supreme amongst the medieval routes was the journey to the shrine of St James, the brother of Jesus, at Compostela in Northern Spain, making its way across central and southern France. The pilgrims' token (parallel to the Becket medallion given at Canterbury) received by the weary travellers on reaching their destination, the scallop shell, has become the universal symbol of pilgrimage. Undoubtedly, the presence of relics (however well attested) was essential to the development of the cult of a saint and thus of significant pilgrim centres. This was true of Compostela itself, of the shrine of Benedict at St-Benoit-sur-Loire at Fleury in France, or indeed of Canterbury, Durham or Lincoln. In Lincoln, just in front of the ruined shrine of St Hugh of Avalon, the pavement is scooped out through the action of myriad pilgrims genuflecting before the saint's relics. Where relics were not venerated the focus might be upon a vision of Our Lady as at Walsingham and later Lourdes.

It is easy to assume that with the ending of the Middle Ages, with the growth of new learning following the Renaissance, and particularly following the Reformation, that pilgrimage would lose its power to attract the mind and heart. Certainly, both the Reformation and the Enlightenment, in different ways, served to undermine the cult of the saints, the veneration of relics and the honouring of visions which had often formed part of the focus for medieval pilgrims. The Reformers sought to drive out idolatry; the writers of the Enlightenment effectively undermined what they believed to be superstition. The broader understanding of pilgrimage, however, which used the term as a way of understanding one's life, remained an image rich in its resonances.

One of the most irascible and pungent of the Puritan writers in England, John Bunyan, allowed the image to shape his most influential work, *Pilgrim's Progress*. It is also, of course, the dominant theme in his most famous lyric (from the same book):

There's no discouragement
Shall make him once relent
His first avowed intent
   To be a pilgrim.

Pilgrim's Progress allows none of the ingredients of this now venerable tradition to be lost upon the way. Within the compass of a panoramic allegory, the landscape, the buildings and the terrain have themselves become part of the treasury of the English literary landscape. The Slough of Despond, Doubting Castle and the Land of Beulah combine with the characters who Christian meets on the way. Some of them – Apollyon, for example – were hazards to Christian's progress. The Bishop of Rome was certainly not depicted as Christian's strongest supporter, although by Bunyan's time the menace of international popery was less of a threat:

> Giant Pope is by reason of age, and also of the many shrewd brushes that he met in his younger days, grown so crazy and stiff in his joints, that he can now do little more than sit in his cave's mouth, grinning at Pilgrims as they go by, and biting his nails because he cannot come at them.

It was hardly an ecumenical age! Others, like Faithful and Valiant for Truth, supported Christian on his journey. The conclusion of the journey is one of assurance: 'Tell them [his family] moreover of my present blessed condition, and of my happy arrival at the Celestial City.'

It was not, however, only in the realms of the intensely religious where the image of pilgrimage was preserved. Even in those circles where scepticism was making itself manifest the image was used for the life of the individual. Sir Walter Ralegh in his 'The Passionate Man's Pilgrimage' presses many of the familiar elements into service. The terrain, sustenance for the journey, adequate attire, and even the Compostela medallion – all are there. It is a fairly lonely journey and none of Chaucer's ribald characters make an appearance, but Ralegh's lines remain interesting in showing how the theme of the spiritual journey had now taken firm root in the soul of humankind.

Give me my scallop-shell of quiet,
My staff of faith to walk upon,
My scrip of joy, immortal diet,
My bottle of salvation,
My gown of glory, hope's true gage,
And thus I'll take my pilgrimage.

The journey of Gerontius in *The Dream of Gerontius*, written by John Henry Newman in 1865 and formed into an oratorio by Edward Elgar in 1899–1900, demonstrates the power of the image and roots it unforgettably within a Christian understanding of human existence. Although the imagery is largely traditional, there is a profound affirmation of the Christian way during an age of increasing uncertainty and scepticism.

Gathering up these preliminary historical reflections, we can see how pilgrimage has remained both a practical expression of religious faith and also an image applied down the ages to the journey of human life and existence. It is not solely a medieval and Catholic concept, either in its practical or in its figurative use. In this it may have sharp lessons for us, as we seek to learn more of and benefit from both the theme of pilgrimage and the roots of our own tradition in these islands. What precisely might those lessons be?

PILGRIMS THROUGH LIFE

In the second half of this chapter we shall explore the essential elements experienced in pilgrimage and reflect upon their significance in our understanding of the Christian life. In our age, which is classically an age of nostalgia, it is all too easy for pilgrimage to be seen through wistful, antique lenses. It was not so in the tradition. An essential element of the pilgrim's journey has been the looking forward. In glancing ahead to the coming journey there are perhaps six essential elements which if ignored reduce the richness of the experience and may even deflect us from or inhibit us in our journey.

The journey begins on our own home territory – our roots are of seminal importance. Then secondly there are the people who accompany us along the pilgrims' way. Thirdly there is the matter of our sustenance on the journey, and fourthly a recognition of the uniqueness of the terrain we are crossing. Finally we must retain a vision for our arrival and of the promise of God on reaching our destination.

It is the significance of our roots, an understanding of our material and spiritual home, which is the substance of our second chapter. But what might this mean more generally in our understanding of the Christian life? We can understand our spiritual and material roots in a purely individualistic manner. Starting from here, we are faced with an incorrigible plurality. None of us is the same as any other. Some will be Christians by nurture, others through dramatic conversion. Some will have been brought up on the noise of the inner city and others in the relative peace of the countryside. But each of us is also the daughter or son of a tradition. Whether they are in Methodism, Anglicanism or the Roman Catholic Church, those roots shape our growth. The Covenant Service and Wesley's hymns have enriched the lives of those of the Methodist tradition – and indeed of others too. The patterns of church government found in Presbyterianism and other reformed churches have shaped something of our attitudes to democracy and also of our appreciation of local traditions.

Within these islands, however, there are roots which go deeper still into our history and which we all share. The history which Bede recounts in his remarkable *Ecclesiastical History of the English People* is a history shared by all English people, and indeed through its accounts of our Celtic and Roman roots by all of us in our four nations. To visit the ancient Christian sites at Kells in Ireland, at Whithorn in Galloway, at St Davids in Wales or at Bradwell in Essex is to unearth something of the Christian heritage which has shaped us all. It is a common well from which we have all drunk, often without realizing it. A deeper appreciation of the history of these foundations and of the faith which inspired them will direct our glance forward as well as backward. It will shape our own response to faith in God. It will direct our service to the world.

PEOPLE ALONG THE WAY

It is perhaps the people whom the pilgrims meet along the way who are most memorable of all in Chaucer's *Canterbury Tales*. Each of the tales is told around a significant character. Chaucer spares nothing in offering a realistic and sometimes less than attractive picture of those who shared the journey. Take, for example, the Prioress as she is described in the *General Prologue*:

> There also was a Nun, a Prioress,
> Her way of smiling very simple and coy.
> Her greatest oath was only 'By St Loy!'
> And she was known as Madam Eglantyne.

And well she sang a service, with a fine
Intoning through her nose, as was most seemly,
And she spoke daintily in French, extremely,
After the school of Stratford-atte-Bowe;
French in the Paris style she did not know.

Chaucer does not conceal his irony. It remains a fact that our companions on the way are often not those whom we would have chosen. The Church is always a microcosm of humanity. It is both a human and a divine institution. Although Christ is its head it collects together all souls of sinful humanity.

Despite the Church's imperfections, however, community has been an essential part of its character through the ages; the body of Christ is itself a corporate image. So many of those ancient sites that we might visit in Britain and Ireland are the visible remains of human communities. The different patterns that we shall explore in chapters three and four are formed through the existence of different communities moulded by different landscapes, different experiences and different cultural expressions. The contradictions, collisions and disagreements described in our fifth chapter are the attempts of those communities to come to understand each other and ultimately to live together as one holy catholic and apostolic Church. Our own experience of being part of a Christian community will itself also have been mixed. It is easy to become either cynical about its failings, or unrealistic about its perfectibility. The model of pilgrimage is a realistic model, but it also implies positive development as we move forward together. Chaucer's irony implies an acceptance of the Prioress even in those attributes he least admires.

FOOD FOR THE JOURNEY

Sustenance for the journey is an essential element within pilgrimage which takes us firmly back into the world of the Bible. Israel's journey through the wilderness with Moses was sustained at one point through manna from heaven (Exodus 16:14 ff.). The narrative here implies more than simple food for the body; the survival of the Israelites was dependent upon God. Many of the historical books of the Old Testament and indeed a number of the Psalms chronicle God's care for his people. Israel's history was a history of salvation. In the New Testament too there is often reference to spiritual nourishment. In the Temptations of Jesus (Matthew 4:4; Luke 4:4) we are reminded that 'man cannot live by bread alone'. Early on in the history of the Church, the eucharist becomes the spiritual food of the Christian community. St Paul is at pains to make clear the difference between material and spiritual food (1 Corinthians 1:20 ff.).

This essential spiritual food which nourishes us along the way is not only offered through the sacraments, but also, as the gospel notes, 'through every word that comes from the mouth of God'. Holy Scripture and Christian teaching nourish the pilgrim along the way. The Christian Church has not always been effective at reminding us of the complementarity of word and sacrament. Indeed it is easy to allow different traditions of teaching to supplant one another instead of coming together to enrich the life of the Church. The coming together of the Celtic and Roman traditions offered just such an enrichment, and yet they were easily perceived as being opposed to each other. The local and the universal each offer something to the community and to the Christian soul as we shall discover in our sixth chapter. Sustenance for the Christian way, like any other form of food, calls for a varied and balanced diet.

The more material parallels in medieval and contemporary patterns of pilgrimage are obvious in the hostelries and inns which offer food and rest along the way. Chaucer's tales begin in 'The Tabard' at Southwark, 'where they made us easy, all was of the best'.

LANDSCAPE AND TERRAIN

Chaucer is equally graphic in his description of the terrain encountered on the journey and the places through which his pilgrims travelled:

Don't you all know where there stands a little town,
The one that people call Bob-up-and-down,
Near Blean Woods on the way to Canterbury?
Well, it was thereabouts our Host turned merry.
'Dun's in the mire!' he said. 'Behold King hog;
For love or money drag him from his bog!'

Clearly on this occasion our pilgrim's experience of the terrain was exaggerated by the degree of his inebriation. Chaucer's recognition of the changing landscape and of the character of the hamlets and towns through which these medieval Christians would pass indicated, as ever, sharp powers of observation.

The parallels with our contemporary religious experience are obvious. Our daily lives are filled with variety of terrain – we continually experience changes in our moods, our circumstances and our surroundings. Often, people are brought to faith through what are sometimes called 'limit experiences' – experiences which either challenge our mortality, or broaden our perspective on human existence. There is the story of the woman who saw a child run out in front of her car while playing in the

19

road. As a driver, she was powerless to stop, and the child was killed instantly. The extraordinary generosity and forgiveness of the parents, despite their grief, so challenged the car driver that she was brought to that same conviction of faith present in the forbearing parents.

But it will not always be tragedy which challenges people to review their lives in the light of Christian faith. It may simply be the remarkable transparency of the life of a particular individual or group to the grace of God, which effectively contains its own power to convert. Such encounters will not always issue in such positive responses. Tragedy and apparently meaningless suffering can atrophy or destroy religious faith as well as stimulate it. The world is not always easy to read, even through the eyes of faith. Our earthly pilgrimage contains as many ambiguities and ironies as does the wry account of the fate of medieval pilgrims in Chaucer's memorable tales.

A VISION FOR THE JOURNEY

The existence of such ambiguity makes the keeping of the vision for one's arrival an essential part of the pilgrims' supplies. Medieval spirituality allowed for the building of cathedrals and for the production of works of art 'to the greater glory of God'. Those cathedrals which formed the focus for pilgrimage also presented the weary traveller with a dazzling vision in preparation for her final arrival. Often this would be true of both the interior or exterior of the building. At Canterbury, the apotheosis of perpendicular gothic is seen in the nave vaulting and in the lofty Bell Harry Tower. At Durham, the massive Romanesque pillars of the nave and the great central tower similarly present the pilgrim with a powerful vision. Shrines to Becket in Canterbury, to Cuthbert in Durham or to Hugh in

Lincoln would have been splendid and colourful. The eye of the pilgrim would be fixed with a steady gaze.

This image has also remained central to the Christian life when seen as pilgrimage. Classically it was set out by Kenneth Kirk in his classic *The Vision of God*. Kirk shows how if the Christian soul sets his eyes on the vision of God it has the power to transform not only patterns of prayer, but also human behaviour. Individuals are taken out of themselves, 'unselfed', and freed to relate to God.

> What is clear is that Christianity came into a world tantalized with the belief that some men at least had seen God, and found in the vision the sum of human happiness; a world aching with hope that the same vision was attainable by all.

Such a possibility is made available to us all through the incarnation of God in Jesus Christ. There is the reality of an immediate relationship with God. So Kirk writes again:

> This means to say that Jesus, though He spoke little about 'seeing God', brought God more vividly before the spiritual eyes of His contemporaries than any other has ever done. 'He gave a vision of God where others could only speak of it!'[3]

This vision which gives purpose and direction to the journey is what gives priority for the Christian to a moral response to God's grace. It is also that which attracts the soul to the life of prayer, worship and contemplation. The eighth and ninth chapters of this book will focus upon these elements within the vision that directs our pilgrimage. We shall see how the tradition informs our perception of that vision.

JOURNEY'S END

Our final chapter is styled 'A Living Pilgrimage'. Christianity has always cherished the past, lived out its witness in the present and looked to the future in God. Living pilgrimage means that we are bidden to live our lives with a view to the future in God. A book focusing on the medieval cult of the saints, published a few years ago, began: 'This book is about the joining of Heaven and Earth ...' People have also described the richness of the liturgy as celebrated in the Orthodox tradition as experiencing a little bit of heaven on earth. Since Christian faith has always affirmed the world, however, our thanksgiving and hope for the future are not purely set on the heavenly plane. Our concern with a moral vision and the transformation of a fallen and fragmented world are reminders of this. The eucharist itself looks forward and so is a banquet which offers us a glimpse of the world fulfilled in God. It is both the pilgrims' food and the pilgrims' promise.

Our reflections have shown us then how the experience of pilgrimage as captured in medieval times and since, and the understanding of Christian life as pilgrimage remain powerful images and aids in our contemporary world. There remains a restlessness within the human soul which, as with the Celtic missionaries of old, entices us away from our security and that which we know, to journey in search of something deeper. Particular places and people have focused pilgrimage down the ages and they will focus our journey through the coming pages. Becket and Canterbury have set us on our way. We have been reminded of the significance of our roots, of the variety of the terrain, of the vision of God which directs us, of the promise to which we are called and of the sustenance of worship and prayer which nourishes us on our way.

For Meditation

Prayer the Churches banquet, Angels age,
Gods breath in man returning to his birth,
The soul in paraphrase, heart in pilgrimage,
The Christian plummet sounding heav'n and earth;

Engine against th' Almightie, sinners towre,
Reversed thunder, Christ-side-piercing spear,
The six-daies world-transposing in an houre,
A kinde of tune, which all things heare and fear;

Softnesse, and peace, and joy, and love, and blisse,
Exalted Manna, gladnesse of the best,
Heaven in ordinarie, man well drest,
The milkie way, the bird of Paradise,

Church-bels beyond the starres heard, the souls bloud,
The land of spices; something understood.

George Herbert

TWO

NURTURING OUR ROOTS

We explore the early history of Christianity in Britain and Ireland and in doing so see the importance of cherishing our distinctive heritage.

BEDE'S HISTORY

Pilgrims treading the path to the ancient site of Benedict Biscop's monastery at Jarrow will find themselves in a rather different and more ambiguous environment on their arrival there than is often the case with the isolated monastic sites of mediaeval England, with their neatly trimmed grass verges. For the monastery that contained the scriptorium of the Venerable Bede, author of the earliest extant history of England, is set against a mixed backcloth of decayed and decaying industry and marshy riverside wasteland which may appear little different now to the natural landscape over which Bede himself looked.

The pilgrimage is worthwhile as much for this unusual texture of conflicting images as it is for sight of the remnants of the ancient monastery. The town of Jarrow is patterned by the familiar intermingling of modern shopping parades and tower blocks. The twentieth century is never far away: the approach roads to the Tyne road tunnel dominate the landscape. On the riverside, the twentieth century is also abundantly in evidence. Oil storage tanks jostle with the gaunt structures of the nearby industrial estate, itself dedicated to the memory of Bede, the venerable pioneer of historical research. Perhaps most poignant of all are the sites of the shipyards which died in the early 1930s, where the landscape in places has slid back to look little different to the surviving natural phenomenon of the swampy Jarrow Slake. It was the death of the shipyards which led to one of the most famous of modern secular pilgrimages in the form of the Jarrow hunger marches of the mid-1930s. Unemployed shipyard workers made their way down to Westminster to make their plight (and the plight of many like them in other industries) plain to their Member of Parliament, in order that the politicians might not stand idly by.

Despite all these signs of continuing decay and radical change, the evidence of the existence of those scholarly monks of the seventh century remains. Although the church is much restored, with a Victorian nave by Sir Gilbert Scott, the chancel, which was the nave of the Saxon church (albeit from after Bede's time), survives. Recent excavation has revealed the strong walls of a monastic house on the site of the place to which Bede came at the age of twelve, and in which same place he died in 735, just four years after the completion of his *Ecclesiastical History*.

Bede's *History* is written in excellent Latin; he was a scholar-monk and effectively his life's experience was largely that of the library and the scriptorium. As a local boy – there is little evidence that he travelled often or widely – Lindisfarne and York were probably the farthest extents of his expeditions and explorations into the wider world. Nevertheless, his *History* is far from being exclusively pious and churchy in its feel. A panorama of the politics and conflicts of the Anglo-Saxon courts is interwoven with the miraculous and the religious. Hermits and missionaries make their appearance, but it is within a rich tapestry of human commerce and intercourse. In that sense, the extraordinary landscape surrounding his monastic house in twentieth-century Britain reflects the unavoidable interrelationship of the holy and the secular, even if Bede's style and background imply a rather more stable and tranquil world than that within which he actually lived.

The antiquity of Bede's *History* and the style of his writing should not put off the modern reader. The panoramic nature of his *History* has already been described. The writing is vivid and the catalogue of saints and martyrs, heroines and heroes, kings and queens, is a true introduction to the roots of Christianity in our islands. At times the miraculous overtakes one to a fantastic degree, and on other occasions the detail can appear to be overwhelming. In total, however, the historical landscape is clear and Bede's own preferences project sharply through the intervening twelve and a half centuries since he wrote. Albeit sometimes with an all too obvious bias in the story-telling, the roots of our society and of our religious institutions shine through with extraordinary clarity.

A visit to the deadlands of the South Tyne estuary repays the time spent. Hartlepool, Wearmouth and Jarrow, all sites of Anglo-Saxon monasteries, all contain that potent mixture of the holy site with the power, ugliness, and often desolation of an industrial and post-industrial landscape. Lindisfarne and Whitby retain some of their sense of isolation, an isolation perfectly preserved in the ruined hermits' cells of the Farnes and of Coquet Island. Almost by accident, this kaleidoscope of landscapes reminds us of the rich tapestry of early Christian pilgrimage. The pattern of mission combined with prayer – an oscillation between activity and withdrawal – these remind the modern pilgrim of the tension that lies at the heart of the gospel. It was there in the cities of the ancient world and with the monks of the Egyptian desert. Early Christian sites in our islands reflect similar roots to those discovered throughout the world of Christian antiquity.

UNCOVERING ROOTS

Edward White Benson, Archbishop of Canterbury from 1883 to 1896, instructed Arthur Mason to write a book (which was eventually published after Benson's death) to commemorate the thirteen hundredth anniversary of Augustine's arrival in 597. It must consist, he wrote, of 'a complete collection of authentic documents bearing on Augustine's coming' which should be accompanied by 'investigations on the spot, geographic and hydrographic ... [at] ... Ebbsfleet and at Richborough', and by 'essays short and few, shewing the real bearing of the events on later controversy'. Benson's request was for nothing more or less than an uncovering of the roots of the mission of St Augustine to England.

Some would argue that the significance of roots, of tradition and history, was better appreciated in the time of Benson than it is now. Certainly, a historical consciousness is now often lacking within Christianity. The importance of the critical study of history has increased but there is now less enthusiasm in some circles for roots and for antiquity; such a preoccupation, it is argued, leads to traditionalism and antiquarianism. The Church is already the final bastion of tradition and conservatism; it needs no help to take it further in that direction. Interestingly enough, however, the rise of critical historical study has had revolutionary rather than conservative effects. The discovery of the process whereby things came to be can be both relativizing and unnerving. We would often rather believe that things have always been so. But an understanding of how our traditions have been shaped can be refreshing, illuminating and invigorating.

Our initial reflections on pilgrimage pointed to the significance of our roots; we are all daughters and sons of a tradition. Our history shapes our present response. Sometimes that history makes us resistant to change. Bishops often testify to the difficulty of bringing together two villages as one parish, since one village supported the King and the other Parliament during the English Civil War. Earlier this century in China, someone was heard to ask: 'Are you used to strangers in these parts?' 'Ah yes,' was the answer, 'the Mongols passed by this village in the thirteenth century.'

Our roots often run very deep, and the examination of documents and the excavation of archaeological sites has helped enormously in our understanding of our Christian origins; in the Celtic period it is archaeology which is of first significance. Bede's *History* is the first real encounter with research and chronicling, using source documents, and the folk memories of his fellow men and women.

THE MAKING OF A CIVILIZATION

Britain, like most cultures, is the result of a series of migrations of peoples both in the period of antiquity and later. Bede describes the waves of invasions of Britain in his own characteristically measured tones; somehow the conflict and violence is softened:

> In [this] time the Angles and Saxons came to Britain at the invitation of King Vortigen in three long-ships ...

Despite it being by invitation,

> They engaged the enemy advancing from the north, and
> having defeated them, sent back news of their success to
> their homeland, adding that the country was fertile and the
> Britons cowardly.

Bede was never at pains to protect the Britons from invective.
Religiously, they had shown themselves, he believed, to be
obtuse and heterodox. Such slights on their character as we
encounter here in Bede's history were used to reinforce his
tendentious account of their religious life. Bede was, however,
clear about the influence and power of the alien invaders:

> These new-comers were from the three most formidable races
> of Germany, the Saxons, Angles, and Jutes ... It was not long
> before such hordes of these alien peoples vied together to
> crowd into the island that the natives who had invited them
> began to live in terror.

Certainly, the successive invasions from the east had two particularly seminal effects upon Britain. First of all, the unity and
order placed upon the province by the Romans was destroyed.
Bede was aware of the positive effects of the Pax Romana and
of the corrosive effects of a collapse of unity and order. The
period of chaos that ensued is well described in his commentary on the conflicts between the Anglo-Saxon kingdoms. Secondly, it is clear that Christianity had arrived in Britain during
the Roman period and that the series of pagan invasions did
much to uproot and atrophy the growth of this tender plant.

The later migrations and assaults should also not be seen as
pagan precursors to the D-Day landings. The arrivals were
generally of small parties of adventurers rather than concerted

invasions. It was around the year 600 that the kingdoms catalogued in Bede's *History* began to take their shape. Many kingdoms are mentioned, although it is perhaps the two in Northumbria and that in Mercia which were most formative in the early history of English Christianity. The conversion of the Anglo-Saxons was not particularly swift, and attitudes to the old religions varied markedly between the missionaries. Some would rigorously destroy the pagan temples and their artefacts; elsewhere a more gradual approach would prevail – Aidan's pillar would replace that of Thor. That part of the church in Bamburgh against which Aidan leaned at the time of his death was later venerated and brought inside the enlarged church. Pagan sanctuaries thus became Christian shrines.

Despite the instability of this period, the earlier British Christianity did survive. There are tell-tale signs, such as place names which contain 'eccles' (Eccles, Egglescliffe), a direct link with the Welsh eglwys meaning 'church'. Even dioceses survived in Whithorn and Carlisle, proving that British Christianity was not purely monastic, as some have argued. Furthermore, in the past, historians argued that all the British were pushed westwards by successive invasions, to inhabit what is now Wales, Cornwall, and western Cumbria. (Ireland was already peopled by those of Celtic origin, probably having arrived originally from Spain.) But Britons survived also in Kent and in Northumbria, although the survival of Britons did not necessarily mean the survival of Christianity; this was more likely to be the case in towns of Roman origin.

The links with mainland Europe were understandably very considerable. It was not only the German and Scandinavian roots of the Saxons or the Vikings. The Celtic Britons who are often seen as the original occupants of our islands were themselves descendants of earlier waves of invasions. We have referred already to the emigration from Spain to Ireland. The

Celts were originally northern, and perhaps slightly eastern, neighbours to the Greek and Roman Empires. *Keltoi* meant simply 'strangers'. Celtic art can thus be traced to the eastern Mediterranean and to other parts of Europe as well as in Britain and Ireland. Different invasions brought Celtic culture and language to Ireland and the Isle of Man and to Brittany, Cornwall, and Wales. These different migrations gave issue to the contrasting languages/cultures which developed in these different parts of Britain, Ireland, and France. It is always dangerous, of course, to place too much faith in archaeological co-incidences as the basis for ethnic migration routes. At times such links are equally explicable through trade routes and even more occasional cross-cultural links. One must proceed with a similar caution in respect of religious links. Some of the Celtic migrations probably arrived in these islands six or seven hundred years before the birth of Christ; their pilgrimages were certainly pre-Christian.

THE FLAVOUR OF CIVILIZATION

Bede's *History* was inevitably a product of its age. Not only did it bring with it Bede's own preoccupations, it was flavoured by the cultural assumptions of the times. The religious culture was similarly conditioned. There was a clear sense of the imminent coming of the end; it was a religion with an apocalyptic stamp. Pope Gregory the Great's letter to King Ethelbert allows the Bible to lose none of its urgency in its more millenarian passages:

We would also have Your Majesty know what we have learned from the words of Almighty God in Holy Scripture, that the end of this present world is at hand and the everlasting

Kingdom of Saints is approaching. When the end of the world is near, unprecedented things occur – portents in the sky, terrors from heaven, unseasonable tempests, waves, famines, pestilences, and widespread earthquakes. Not all these things will happen during our own lifetimes, but will all ensue in due course.

At times, of course, events within and between nations conspired to heighten this sense of the imminent end of all things. It was from amidst such conditions that the biblical apocalyptic material was originally provoked. Palestine was frequently a theatre of war; there was thus a prevailing sense of the frailty of our existence and thus of human mortality. One of the most famous passages from Bede's *History* picks up this precise atmosphere. The setting is a meeting of King Edwin of Northumbria's council considering the acceptance of the faith of Christ. It may well have taken place at the king's palace in Ad Gefrin (now Yeavering in Northumberland); archaeological excavations have confirmed the dimensions of the building. Bishop Paulinus is present; Coifi, the chief priest of the traditional religion, has spoken and is now followed by another adviser who remarks:

'Your Majesty, when we compare the present life of man on earth with that time of which we have no knowledge, it seems to me like the swift flight of a single sparrow through the banqueting hall where you are sitting at dinner on a winter's day with your thegns and counsellors. In the midst there is a comforting fire to warm the hall; outside, the storms of winter rain or snow are raging. This sparrow flies swiftly in through one door of the hall, and out through another ... Even so, man appears on earth for a little while; but of what went before this life or of what follows, we know nothing.

Therefore, if this new teaching has brought any more certain knowledge, it seems only right that we should follow it!'

Almost certainly this is a rhetorical passage with an eye to Christian apologetic, but it gives a clear sense of the religious feelings of the time. Similarly one can point to allied attitudes to the miraculous. We have encountered already the transfiguration of the pole of Thor into the holy pillar of Aidan. This accent on miracle (on occasions what we might almost categorize as the fantastic) is again both rhetorical and apologetic and also an indication of the religious culture of the time.

Miraculous tales are there to demonstrate that Christianity is either as potent or more potent than pagan religion. The God of Jesus Christ will heal and bring victory. There was also an allegorical aspect to this emphasis on the miraculous. Men and women were to read more into a particular event than the sheer literal and physical facts. Holy Scripture was similarly interpreted. Miracles bespoke the sanctity and moral probity of holy women and men. Furthermore, the moral rectitude of such men and women enabled humanity to regain a rightful dominion over all creation. Both Aidan and Cuthbert's successor Ethelwald were able to cause the sea to obey them.

There was also the importance of the sources of these stories. Holy men sent them to Bede and expected to find them chronicled clearly in his history. This would not necessarily only be for the kudos it gave to these holy men and women, but also for the spiritual significance of the place or object mentioned. Aidan's pillar is a case in point, as indeed is the reported holiness of the site of Oswald's death:

Many miracles are reported as having occurred at this spot, or by means of the earth taken from it; but I will content myself with two, which I have heard from my elders.

Bede then reports the revival of a sick horse and the curing of a paralytic girl at the place where King Oswald died. A heavenly light is also described as appearing all night over the grave of Oswald, at Bardney Abbey in Lincolnshire. Many of these semi-magical occurrences sometimes make it difficult for us to feel sympathy with the world of Bede, but again we need to find our way back into a time of religious transition and rebirth where all the apologetic and theological instruments of the time were pressed into service. Interestingly enough, miracles of holiness were as possible for a godly king as for a holy hermit.

SACRED AND SECULAR

Remembering Bede's pious and cloistered life, it is remarkable that affairs of state loom as large in his prose as they do. Of course, we cannot compare the affairs of Anglo-Saxon kingdoms with those of a modern nation state, nor the internecine strife between those who were effectively tribal chieftains with the complexities of contemporary international affairs. However, bearing in mind that Bede would himself have worked from source documents or stories told him by other monks and bishops, it is perfectly clear that the sacred and the secular are closely interrelated. Indeed, much of Bede's historical narrative focuses upon the conversion of kings, queens, and royal courts to the Christian faith. The spread of the gospel in Anglo-Saxon times was directly dependent upon the conversion of the powerful. This should hardly surprise us, remembering the effects of the conversion of Constantine upon the fourth-century Roman Empire. The conversion of England was far less systematic simply because there was no longer a Pax Romana. Individual kingdoms would rise and fall and later kings would apostatize and turn their backs upon the new religion.

Bede is aware of the power of the women of the royal courts as well as that of the successful warrior kings. In the account of Augustine's mission, the part of King Ethelbert's wife is a key factor:

> For he had already heard of the Christian religion, having a Christian wife of the Frankish royal house named Bertha, whom he had received from her parents on condition that she should have freedom to hold and practise her faith unhindered with Bishop Liudhard, whom they had sent as her helper in the faith.

Clearly the queen's faith and indeed her relationship to the Frankish court was a matter of some moment. Etheldreda, the queen of King Egfrid of Northumbria, was also quoted as a pious and godly exemplar. She had lived faithfully with the king for twelve years but had preserved the virtue or 'glory' of perpetual virginity. The king (who was her second husband following the death of Tandbert, her first) was understandably less than enthusiastic about her pious self-discipline. Bede writes:

> This fact [her perpetual virginity] is absolutely vouched for by Bishop Wilfrid of blessed memory, of whom I made enquiry when some doubted it. He said that Egfrid promised to give estates and much wealth to him if he could persuade the queen to consummate the marriage, knowing that there was no man for whom she had higher regard.

Etheldreda eventually persuaded the King to give her leave to enter a convent. She became a sister in the convent of Ebba, the King's aunt, at Coldingham in south-eastern Scotland. Later she became an abbess in her own right at Ely.

Bede's account is doubtless not without bias in its description of the relationship between the different royal courts. Indeed, it is equally biased in its dealings with the different Christian missionary traditions. Bede's admiration for the Irish missionaries, for example, cannot be doubted. His loyalty to Rome and its place as the universal focus of unity is, however, equally plain. This dominates Bede's *History* and numerous examples press the point home. His attitude to the revered and beloved Aidan highlights this well:

> His [King Oswald's] request [to the Irish monks] was granted without delay, and they sent him Bishop Aidan, a man of outstanding gentleness, holiness, and moderation. He had a zeal in God, but not according to knowledge, in that he kept Easter in accordance with the customs of his own nation which, as I have several times observed, was between the fourteenth and twentieth days of the moon.

The question of the dating of Easter was one of the key factors of disagreement between the Irish and Roman missionary traditions and was one of the focuses for debate at the Synod of Whitby in 664 where eventually the two traditions were brought into dialogue with each other. The differences and the roots of such contrasts are often used to drive a wedge between the Celtic (Irish) and Roman traditions. As we shall see later, this contrast is often painted with oversimplicity, not allowing for the overlap and interrelation between the traditions. Nevertheless, differences existed and might better be seen in terms of complementarity than conflict. In this way, both sets of roots remain essential to the living Christian tradition in our present age.

BRITISH OR CELTIC OR IRISH

The contrast between the Roman and Celtic ways, focused in the debate over the date of Easter, is one which we shall encounter with more subtlety in the next two chapters. There is, however, need to clarify even at this point the use made of some of the terms. We have already encountered the Celtic tradition and learned something of its roots in mainland Europe. We have seen that the Celtic migrations were spread out over five or six centuries and that these migrations were pre-Christian. We have also seen how the earliest Celtic settlers were not all pushed westward into Cornwall and Wales. The martyrdom of St Alban is a graphic illustration of the survival of Celtic Christianity within the heart of England.

Bede's account places Alban's martyrdom during the reign of the Roman Emperor Diocletian (*c.* 305), although more recent scholarship suggests that it probably occurred earlier in the Roman occupation of Britain. The date now often accepted is *c.* 209, during the time of the Emperor Septimus Severus. Both emperors presided over periods of intense persecution of Christian communities. Bede's account is vivid and shows the Briton, Alban, to be an exemplar of true Christian discipleship during the Roman era. Elsewhere, however, Bede is less enthusiastic about the traditions of British Christianity. Augustine's admonition of the British bishops is sharp and uncompromising. (Historians now place this variously in Bristol, at Aust on the River Severn, and at Great Witley in Worcestershire.) Bede appears to approve of this action. At one point he refers to 'the Britons, who stubbornly preferred their own customs to those in universal use among Christian Churches'. Further on, with reference to King Ethelfrid's defeat of the British at Chester, Bede is still more vilifying in his account, talking of 'the faithless Britons, who had rejected the offer of eternal salvation'.

These encounters with the British Christians in Anglo-Saxon times mean that it is important for us to distinguish carefully the Irish missionaries from the residual British Christians of the earlier period of the Roman occupation. This is not to suggest complete discontinuities within the wider Celtic tradition. It does, however, imply clear distinctions between different groups. These are distinctions that one might expect, remembering the cultural distinctiveness of the various migrant groups, and the complex and varied histories of different parts of Britain and Ireland. It was effectively the Irish and Roman missions, however, that encountered each other at the Synod of Whitby.

PATTERNS OF CIVILIZATION

Geographical shaping of the early Christian patterns was not confined to the routes of migrants, that is, to the pre-Christian pilgrimages of Celtic tribes. History was patterned by the growth of towns or indeed by their absence. Mainland Europe had seen the growth of more urban centres than had burgeoned at this stage in Britain and Ireland. The pattern of Church organization in mainland Europe was therefore rooted in dioceses based on these urban centres. The demographic context was most rural in Ireland, where patterns of mission rooted in monastic foundations tended to be the norm. The character of monastic life in Ireland was itself shaped by the example of hermits and indeed groups of hermits living in the Egyptian desert in earlier centuries. The model was St Anthony of Egypt. In Ireland, and in Northumbria, bishops themselves were based in the monasteries. Such monasteries might well have been established through the pilgrim travels of monks from continental Europe. The presence of pottery of eastern Mediterranean origin does not necessarily imply direct influence on those Irish foundations. They may simply have been presents or the products of trade. Such discoveries do, however, establish clear links between the patterns of monastic life.

In Northumbria, the ecclesiastical structures sometimes – but not always – followed the models established by their Irish forebears. Certainly, Lindisfarne was of this character. One particularly interesting development in this period, under the influence of Wilfrid, was the growth of monastic confederations. These certainly found their origins in the experience of Wilfrid himself at Lindisfarne. Such confederations have recurred throughout history. In later centuries, following the Norman Conquest, different orders based on the rule of St Benedict or of the Cistercians, Augustinians or Premonstratensians grew and thrived. In contemporary times, even within specific orders, houses are often grouped in 'congregations', frequently looking to one specific monastery or abbey as the mother house.

In the monastic confederations, monks moved freely between houses, using each others' facilities, including libraries. They were enriched by mutual experience of each others' traditions: art, worship, contemplative prayer, and scholarship were all held in common. The richness of this culture is also clear from the elaborate jewellery discovered; Cuthbert's pectoral cross is a particularly remarkable example. The *Lindisfarne Gospels* speak of a similar richness, as does the *Book of Kells* in Ireland. One of the best regarded commentators on this period describes Northumbria as a 'crucible of European monasticism'.

THE PATRONAGE AND HOLINESS OF KINGS

We have already discovered the profound intermingling of Church and state which, despite the fragmentation of Britain and Ireland into relatively small kingdoms, played a crucial part in nurturing the spread of the gospel. The presence of the court at Ad Gefrin in Northumbria has been mentioned; later, the court was established in Bamburgh. The patronage of kings was a fact of life both positively and negatively. It was Oswald who requested the Irish monastic foundation in Iona to send Aidan as a missionary to Northumbria. It was King Egfrid who was to expel Wilfrid from his kingdom. Bede describes it thus:

> In the same year [678] a dispute arose between King Egfrid and the most reverend Bishop Wilfrid, who was driven from his diocese, and two bishops were appointed to preside over the Northumbrian people in his place.

It is difficult to ascertain Bede's real attitude toward Wilfrid. He rarely describes him with warmth, although he is generous in his appreciation of his achievements. The *Life* by Eddius is undoubtedly written with an acknowledged positive bias; Wilfrid's trials are described with understanding and compassion and his disagreements with royalty often implied to be due to the whim of sovereigns rather than the brittle behaviour of an imperious prelate. So, Wilfrid is said by Eddius to suffer the persecution of queens as the prophets suffered them. In general, Wilfrid's relationships were happier with the Mercian kings than they were with the rulers of Northumbria.

In the case of Oswald, the King himself is described as a saint. Indeed later he was canonized, and with Aidan and Cuthbert is honoured as one of a trinity of Northumbrian saints from this early period. Apart from the miracles surrounding his grave and place of death, and apart from his calling of the Irish missionaries down from Iona to Northumbria, Oswald's life is depicted as being as pious as it is valorous. Even as he enters battle, he prays to God for heavenly support:

> When King Oswald was about to give battle to the heathens, he set up the sign of the holy cross and, kneeling down, asked God that He would grant his heavenly aid to those who trusted in Him in their dire need.

The battle is itself seen as part of Oswald's discipleship in supporting and spreading the Christian faith. The cross which he used assumes miraculous powers. Numerous people are cured by it:

> Even to this day many folk take splinters from this holy cross, which they put into water, and when any sick men or beasts drink of it or are sprinkled with it, they are at once restored to health.

Oswald is not the only king to be lauded for his holy and pious life. Indeed, essentially we are brought back to the theme of pilgrimage when we reflect upon the life of Cadwalla, King of the West Saxons and of Coenred, King of the Mercians. Cadwalla abdicated his throne and made pilgrimage to Rome for his baptism. Bede remarks that Cadwalla wished both to be baptized in the city of Saint Peter and Saint Paul and also to die shortly after his baptism; he was granted both requests. Even at this time, the earthly pilgrimage is seen as a figure of the spiritual journey to heaven. Coenred and Offa, Kings of Mercia, not only made their pilgrimage to Rome, but crowned that journey by living their final days in the eternal city as monks.

A EUROPEAN CHURCH

This pattern of royal pilgrimage is just one aspect of a broader mutual influence within European Christianity. Rome was the strongest single influence from mainland Europe, and its significance is never forgotten throughout the pages of Bede's *History*. It was not purely a preoccupation of Bede's. St Columbanus wrote:

> We Irish are especially bound to the See of Peter, and however great and glorious Rome itself may be, it is only this See that is great and renowned for us. The fame of the great city was spread abroad over the rest of the world, but it only reached us when the Chariot of the Church came to us across the western waves with Christ as its charioteer and Peter and Paul as its swift counsels!

Certainly the influence of Rome and its role as a symbol of unity reached a high point during the pontificate of Gregory the Great. His versatility, balance, and humanity avoided stressing the purely juridical aspects of Rome's ecclesiastical power and influence. A wider internationalism existed, however, throughout western Europe; the growth of the monasteries made the significance of external influences more important than ever. Exchange in scholarship and a round of supportive prayer helped enhance intercourse between Britain and Ireland and mainland Europe. Rome was essential in this, but not alone in its influence. The continuation of the Byzantine tradition in the west, particularly in Ravenna, on the eastern seaboard of Italy, meant that the influence of Constantinople and the east continued to filter through to the westernmost parts of Europe.

The traffic was certainly not all one way. Bede makes reference to Pelagius, a British heretic and notorious for his opposition to the teaching on grace by St Augustine of Hippo. There is also reference to a mission to Frisia by St Willibrord and Swidbert. Although not mentioned in Bede, of similar if not greater significance was the mission of St Boniface to Germany. In later centuries, notably the eleventh and twelfth, it was missionaries from England, Scotland, and Ireland who would establish missions in the Scandinavian lands. St Henrik in Finland and St Eric in Sweden continue to be venerated as the missionaries who brought the gospel to those lands. The broad European roots of Christianity can be traced back to this early period. They are roots that we too rarely remember and cherish.

One of the remarkable facets not only of Bede's *Ecclesiastical History* but of so many of the roots of Christianity in these islands, is the inextricable connection between Ireland, Britain, and mainland Europe. Pilgrimage and mission had become integrally related and complex mutual patterns of influence can be traced. It is easy to suggest that the gospel is acculturated to such a degree that regional roots are made to outweigh the significance of wider patterns of influence. As we move on to look in more detail at the Irish and Roman missions, so we shall see how tangled and thus how mutually enriching are these roots.

It is easy for us to seek a pure tradition. Either it is traced to Rome, the eternal city pictured as the source of an unchanging Christian gospel, or it is traced to an idealized Celtic pattern that breathes a liberated and ecologically aware atmosphere direct from the moors of Northumbria or the hills of Ireland. The truth is that we are mongrels and that, since the gospel came to us spreading westwards through the continent, all comes ultimately from mainland Europe. The excitement comes not from drawing simplistic contrasts nor in homogenizing clearly distinct traditions. The excitement and richness is achieved in recognizing these different roots and allowing the still growing plant to benefit from the nourishment of those complementary soils. Cherishing our varied roots will enhance our opportunities to grow in faith.

Prayer

> *O King of glory, Lord of Might,*
> *Who rose today in victory above all the heavens,*
> *Do not leave us orphans,*
> *But send us the Father's promised Spirit of Truth,*
> *Alleluia.*

**Antiphon for *Magnificat* from Vespers of Ascension Day –
quoted in Cuthbert's letter on the illness and death of Bede.**

THREE

CELTIC PATTERNS

The Celtic origins of the Christian mission owe their distinctive flavour to the context in which they flourished – they are an integral part of a wider European tradition.

COLUMBA AND IONA

We were now treading that illustrious Island, which was once the luminary of the Caledonian regions, whence savage clans and roving Barbarians derived the benefits of knowledge, and the blessings of religion ... Whatever withdraws us from the power of our senses, whatever makes the past, the distant, or the future, predominate over the present, advances us in dignity of thinking beings. Far from me, and my friends, be such frigid philosophy as may conduct us indifferent and unmoved over any ground which has been dignified by wisdom, bravery, or virtue. That man is little to be envied, whose patriotism would not gain force upon the plain of *Marathon*, or whose piety would not grow warmer among the ruins of *Iona*.[1]

Samuel Johnson captures with great perceptiveness and immediacy the atmosphere of the Inner Hebridean island of Iona. Even without the powerful magnetism of its religious history,

Iona draws the traveller. The luminosity of its skies; the geological patterns sharpened through the images of the basalt columns of Fingal's Cave on nearby Steffa; the crisp but thermal Atlantic breezes. The short ferry journey from Fionphort on Mull prepares the pilgrim for the remarkable setting of Columba's monastic outpost which, along with Ninian's Whithorn, must be reckoned as one of the cradles of Scottish Christianity. The bay, on the south of the island, where tradition has it Columba landed, remains inviolate and probably looks precisely as it would have done fourteen hundred years ago.

The modern tourist has still more to add to the natural landscape which would have presented itself to Columba. For Iona later became the burial place of kings not only of Scotland and Ireland, but also of Norway; for a short time it became too the site for the cathedral for the bishopric of the Isles. Finally, the energy and vision of George MacLeod, later Lord MacLeod of Fuinary, led to the restoration of the medieval monastic buildings and the establishment of the Iona Community. The influence of the Iona Community's commitment to worship and prayer combined with its steadfast recognition of the social and moral implications of the gospel has been felt throughout the Christian world. The interplay between the gospel and the political realities of human existence, prefigured in the earliest Christian witness within these islands, is powerfully symbolized in the contemporary life of Columba's island.

Although by no means the earliest saint from our Celtic Christian past – both Ninian and Patrick were born in the fourth century – Columba remains the most powerful symbolic focus for that tradition; his Irish roots, his pilgrimage to Scotland and the mission to the English (albeit after his death) which sprang from Iona at the behest of King Oswald of Northumbria serve to capture within one man the far-reaching influence of Celtic patterns of monasticism, spirituality, and ecclesiology.

Columba, or Colmcille as he is sometimes known, was born in the year 521 in the hamlet of Garton near Letterkenny in Donegal. He was a scion of the princely family O'Neill and the kings of Leinster; Columba, then, was of royal birth and of the same family as the High King. He became a monk and monastic pioneer, beginning at Derry; Derry still sees Columba as its founding father.

Columba's history was one of political involvement and even conflict. Christianity in Ireland had been planted only a century earlier and it remained a frail organism. Columba was instrumental in the defeat of the High King – another O'Neill – and thus in the advance against paganism. Some argue that Columba's political engagement was the ultimate reason for his journeying away from his homeland to Iona. It may even have been a self-imposed exile. Much of what we now know of Columba we learn from the pen of Adamnan, one of Columba's successors as abbot and a notable scholar. He wrote his *Life of Columba* almost one hundred years after his master's death.

Columba was not the first Christian colonizer of Iona; there had been a Christian burial place and monastery before him. Nevertheless, on his arrival it became the spiritual centre of the Irish Church and of this particular Celtic Christian tradition. From it, monasteries were founded on other islands and on the mainland. It became something of a bridgehead. Columba had arrived in Iona in 563 and died in 597, the year of Augustine's arrival in Canterbury with his band of Roman monks.

Columba was an exemplar of the Irish monastic tradition. His pattern of life was one of retreat; the monastery in Iona had some elements of the hermitage about it, whilst remaining a centre from which missionaries would be sent out to preach the gospel in the surrounding unfriendly countryside. The parallels with the wilderness tradition and the Desert Fathers are very plain.

The resonant features that have come to be associated with the Celtic roots of Christianity are there in Columba and in the sanctified tradition which flowed from him. He had a feeling for the beauty of nature. Nature is God's and as such is open and transparent to the divine. In Columba's missionary work, prayer, the liturgy and an appreciation of the landscape into which he had been born were integrally related. He was a keen defender of the customs which he had inherited, not least the Celtic observance of the dating for Easter. Iona was famous – or infamous even – in the time of Bede for its heterodoxy on this matter. None the less, Bede was aware of the debt that Northumbrian Christianity owed to Columba and Iona. He wrote:

> Now Columba was the first teacher of the Christian Faith to the Picts living north of the mountains, and founder of the monastery on the Isle of Iona, which long remained venerated by the people of the Picts and the Irish. For this reason, Columba is now known by some people as Columbkill, a name compounded from 'Columba' and 'cell'.

Bede's etymology may now be suspect, but his realization of Columba's seminal role in the Celtic mission is accurate and perceptive. It would be Columba's successors who would set Aidan forth upon his pilgrimage to Northumbria, a pilgrimage which in itself mirrored that of Columba to Iona less than a century earlier.

MISSION OR PILGRIMAGE?

For Irish Christianity, pilgrimage, mission and martyrdom were held closely together; some have described the tradition as 'travelling for the sake of Christ'. The common ground between martyrdom and pilgrimage emphasizes the fact that for Irish monks the key reasoning behind travelling to a distant land was ascetic rather than missionary. Monks would travel out into the unknown and found a monastery in the wilderness. Columba in Iona, and Aidan and then later Cuthbert on Lindisfarne and the Farne Islands are later exemplars of this tradition.

In this case, should we not see Columba's journeying as primarily a missionary journey? There is a danger in placing upon the Celtic communities templates and patterns which originate from a later period, and which may offer distinctions which are too hard and fast between mission and the eremitic life. Contemplative houses of prayer, hermitages, and monasteries often gather to themselves pilgrims, seekers and searchers after the truth. Undoubtedly people come to the gospel by such means; in that sense, the ascetic and often tough pilgrimages of the Irish monks were often missionary. Columba's mission to Iona may be an unusual and even idiosyncratic case, where the original intentions were primarily missionary. For Iona was just off the coast of the realm of King Brude. The King had to be converted if the monastery and Christian faith were to survive.

So, pilgrimage and mission were often fairly closely caught up with each other. The extensive pilgrim journeys of the early Irish monks played a significant part in bringing Christianity to Europe. Contacts existed not only between Ireland, Scotland, and England, but also more widely. Patrick journeyed from Britain to Ireland. The Celtic traditions of Cornwall, Wales, and Brittany benefited from a wealth of cross-fertilization. St Non, the mother of St David, probably originated in northwest France; there is evidence of her, too, at Altarnun in Cornwall; St Non's well on the edge of St Davids in south-west Wales also relates to the saintly matron's wanderings. Patterns of Celtic civilization throughout Europe provide evidence both for the continental spread of Christianity and for the Celtic monastic tradition's part within this.

CELTIC CHRISTIANITY IN CONTEXT

The rediscovery of Celtic patterns of Christian spirituality has coincided with a renewal of regional and national enthusiasms for the specifics of individual cultures. The clear identification of early Irish Christianity in particular with 'the land and the landscape' has further enhanced the attractiveness of Celtic patterns for modern Christian people. It is important, however, to guard against exaggerated and indeed inaccurate contrasts. Roman and Celtic patterns are too easily placed alongside each other as incompatible alternatives. The comprehensive inter-weaving of traditions across Europe, however, does not allow for such a simplistic contrast. St Patrick is a useful case in point. Patrick lived from about 389 until 461; he was the son of a Romano-British deacon and the grandson of a priest. Celtic traditions remained strong at this time in Britain and, at the age of forty-five, Patrick was sent in 432 to evangelize Ireland. It is likely that he was sent to *organize* the Church there; Christianity came to Ireland too from other parts of Britain and from mainland continental Europe. Despite his Celtic (British) roots, Patrick was a thoroughly 'Roman' Christian. He had been educated using the Latin Bible and he handed on Latin culture. The Church which was Patrick's legacy to Ireland was served largely by secular clergy rather than monks. It was ruled over by a local bishop in the style of mainland Europe, where episcopal sees were based on local cities.

In Ireland, however, Christianity had to adapt to a different culture. There were no towns or cities and ultimately the spread of Christianity would perforce depend upon the establishment of monasteries and a 'minster' pattern of evangelism. Monks would journey out from the minster (minster was simply the Old English word for monastery) and act as missionaries to the surrounding countryside. Cuthbert adopted a similar style in seventh-century Northumbria. In Patrick's mission, Roman and Celtic (British in this case) patterns were closely interwoven. There were distinctions, but they did not stand in opposition to each other. Instead, the characteristics of a particular Church related understandably to the context out of which it grew. Even the term 'Celtic' may be a dangerously general term. Different Celtic Christians would develop different patterns of spiritual life. In parts of Europe where there were urban centres, there the pattern of a local bishop using secular clergy for mission might well prevail. The context was the clue.

In Ireland the context was quite different. It was rural and it was pagan. Both these factors were crucial and may well have influenced the patterns of Christian observance that we now broadly associate with the adjective 'Celtic'. Indeed, the Irish story is the most illuminating case of Celtic culture and religion (often pre-Christian) and Christianity interrelating with each other to produce a new synthesis. Patrick's own synthesis already included elements of Celtic culture within it. In Ireland, however, he engaged with and indeed aggressively challenged paganism; he reacted to those who worshipped the sun or idols and who practised magic, including the Druids. Patrick encountered a wealth of Celtic deities.

On occasions the synthesis resulting from Christian mission was dramatic. A vivid example was the case of Brigid. Brigid was the daughter of the Celtic high-god Daghda. She was a mother goddess and was associated with the arts of healing and handiwork. But Brigid (453–523) was also an early Irish saint and the founder of a double community for sisters and for monks in Kildare; the present Church of Ireland cathedral in the centre of the town of Kildare stands on the site of the monastery. St Brigid was famous for her hospitality and for her healing ministry. Many miracles were told of her and there are clear links between the later Brigidine traditions and those of the earlier pagan mother-goddess. One writer puts it thus: 'Clearly the worship of the Celtic goddess Brigid was so deep-rooted and this matriarchal figure so strong that she could not be driven out by the Christian Church, which had to take her over'.[2] The later importance of Brigid as one of the most pre-eminent of Irish saints, indeed one of the patrons of Ireland, is clear evidence of the importance of strong and saintly women in the Celtic tradition. The heroic Celtic culture accepted and embraced women.[3] These pages have been peppered with the names of powerful and godly queens and matrons.

Associations of *place* exist in Ireland too. The great double monastery at Kildare was set up at a former Celtic sanctuary; Kildare means the 'church of the oak'. The cathedral in Armagh almost certainly stood on the site of or near to a pagan sanctuary, possibly with druidic connections. It is also the case that the sacred places of the pagan cults were directly converted into Christian shrines and holy places. At Menhir ut Brigognan, in Finistère, Brittany, the so-called 'wonderful stone' is a pre-Christian megalith upon the top of which stands an early Breton cross. On some of these megaliths or menhirs the sun remains the main motif to be engraved. On occasions the sun remains at the centre with cruciform leaves issuing around it. Understandably, many believe this pattern to be the forerunner of the later Irish Christian solar cross, where cross and sun effectively merge in the familiar pattern of that which is often simply referred to as a Celtic cross. Early Irish Christianity emphasized worship of the victorious risen Christ who rules over the earth and the human race as radiantly as the sun.

Other links between the earlier pagan culture and religion

existed. Attitudes to nature which later became associated with Celtic Christianity can partially be traced to such roots. Celtic and Christian traditions also conjoin in Arthurian legend. Such reflections should not lead us to despise these early Christian/Celtic roots. Study of the New Testament and of the early Fathers makes it clear how Christianity has accommodated itself to the culture in which it finds itself. T. S. Eliot wrote: 'Christianity is always adapting itself into something which can be believed'. Celtic accommodation is but one example of how the Christian gospel was affected by the context in which it grew. It is an elementary lesson of apologetics. The example of Patrick shows how Christian missionaries often allowed themselves a lively engagement with the surrounding culture. The Celtic pattern of Christian observance should not be seen as hostile to culture. The examples of Celtic missionaries building upon pagan foundations we have looked at testify to this. Irish monasticism continued to affirm the goodness of creation and in doing so found itself consistent with the attitudes of the pagan traditions it supplanted. Part of the success of the Celtic mission may have been its ability to graft the essence of the Christian gospel on to the traditions, sanctuaries, and festivals it encountered. Christian faith was not compromised but contextualized. That was part of the genius of those who were missionaries throughout our islands. It was also part of what gave Celtic Christianity its unique character whilst remaining within the mainstream of European Christianity.

CELTIC MISSION — THE PEOPLE

Celtic Christianity gains its colour and its dynamic from the personalities who shaped it in the early centuries. Notable here are both the Irish missionaries and the missionaries to Ireland.

We have already encountered Patrick and Columba. Earlier we
met with Pelagius, often described as the most famous British
heretic. In this early period two other sanctified characters add
colour to the Celtic canvas. Brendan (*c.* 486–575) was a native
of western Ireland, and if pilgrimage is defined first and foremost by travel, then Brendan was an ardent pilgrim. Branden-
burg, next to Berlin, is named after him, as is a beacon on the
Dutch island of Terschelling; he is said also to have journeyed
in Brittany. The most important monasteries to be associated
with him were closer to his native Kerry – at Annadown,
Inishadroum, and pre-eminently Clonfert. Certainly Brendan
appears to have been a prototype missionary, although it is
notoriously difficult to discern truth from myth; we are too
dependent upon the *Voyage of St Brendan*, which appeared
three hundred years after the death of the saint. His desire for
missionary travel is set out early in the *Voyage*:

> St Brendan chose out fourteen monks from the community,
> shut himself up with them in an oratory, and addressed them
> thus: 'My most beloved co-warriors in spiritual conflict, I beg
> you to help me with your advice, for I am consumed with a
> desire so ardent that it casts every other thought and desire
> out of my heart. I have resolved, if it be God's will, to seek
> out that land of Promise of the Saints which our father
> Barinthus described. What do you think of my plan? Have
> you any advice to offer?'

Whatever may have been their reply, Brendan's own resolve
clearly won through.

> The saintly abbot and his monks spent three months sailing
> hither and thither across the wide expanse of the ocean, and
> all the while they had nothing to look at but sea and sky.

Despite the whimsical, legendary feel of this narrative, both historical hints and the later tradition confirm Brendan's missionary and pilgrim impulses. They also reinforce the trans-European character of Christianity even at this relatively early and missionary stage.

These elements are perhaps even more prominent in the life of Columbanus, sometimes known as Columba the younger. Columbanus was the prototypical pilgrim and missionary saint. Once again, his enthusiasm for 'pilgrimage for Christ' issued from a desire for contemplative solitude. Abraham was his mentor and for Columbanus, as for Abraham, his journeying would require him to live among an alien people. He travelled to mainland Europe, to the Frankish kingdom, founding monasteries in Italy, in Switzerland, and in France. Perhaps most significant of all was his foundation at Bobbio, which would play a seminal part in the battle with the Arian heresy amongst the Lombards. Arianism was a fourth-century heresy which denied the full humanity of Christ, and which persisted in some parts of western Europe into the fifth and sixth centuries. Columbanus reinvigorated the monastic life, and his disciples were described as living under his rule. He is a further testimony to the diverse, trans-European nature of Christianity in the sixth and seventh centuries and of our need to avoid facile contrasts between the Roman and Celtic traditions.

Bede reminds us of this diversity in his *History*. He refers to the Gallican tradition as he reports Augustine of Canterbury's questions to Gregory the Great, and Gregory's answers:

Since we hold the same Faith, why do customs vary in different Churches? Why, for instance, does the method of saying Mass differ in the holy Roman Church and in the Churches of Gaul?

Gregory's answer is both generous and instructive (the emphasis is mine):

> My brother, you are familiar with the usage of the Roman Church, in which you were brought up. But if you have found customs [he would have done in his journeying through Gaul on his journey to England], whether in the Church of Rome and Gaul or any other that may be more acceptable to God, I wish you to make a careful selection of them, and teach the Church of the English, which is still young in the faith, whatever you have been able to learn with profit from the various Churches. *For things should not be loved for the sake of places but places for the sake of good things.*

CELTIC MISSION – THE PATTERNS

Gregory's wise words give us good reason to cherish the rediscovered riches of the Celtic-Irish spiritual and monastic traditions. The Church cannot survive but for the existence of the local congregations of basic eucharistic communities. Equally it will not survive without an increasing blurring of its identity, if there be omitted any reference to the universal, some primacy of honour within a wider context of collegiality and interdependence.

What particular patterns did the early Irish tradition contribute to the broader streams of Christian life?

Certainly the monastic tradition was both different and formative within Irish culture. Without a network of urban centres, the predominant European pattern of episcopal sees was replaced by a network of monasteries where generally the abbot fulfilled the role of the bishop. Monasteries were often built in isolated places, but this did not infer a flight from the world. Instead, this separation was aimed at allowing the monks to offer themselves in service to the rest of humanity. Distinctive traditions developed and they may have been moulded by the culture in which they grew up. The tonsure, for example, which later became characteristic of the clergy of Celtic Christianity, may well derive from the tonsure of the Druids. The local landscape also determined the mission patterns of the Irish monasteries. Ireland had never been part of the Roman Empire; this accounts for the paucity of cities. This lack of urban settlements would have made the parcelling up of the land into parishes serviced by secular priests absurd. The minster pattern offered a pattern of mission well suited to the rural nature of the Irish, Scottish, and indeed Northumbrian landscapes. This is described vividly in Bede's *Life of Cuthbert*. From Lindisfarne, Cuthbert

... continued his custom of frequent visits to the common people in the neighbourhood, in order to rouse them up to seek and to merit the rewards of heaven ... Once when this most holy shepherd of the Lord's flock was doing the round of his sheepfolds, he came into a rough mountain area whither many had gathered from the scattered villages to be confirmed. Now there was no church nor even a place in the mountains fit to receive a bishop and his retinue [Cuthbert was by now a bishop], so the people put up tents for him while for themselves they made huts of felled branches as best they could!

This description of Cuthbert's ministry in Northumbria highlights sharply the closeness of people to the countryside and thus to nature. Here, too, are roots of the love of creation expressed in the Celtic way. Creation is itself blessed; women and men are created by God to act as stewards and priests of his creation. God himself is manifest in the works of his creation. This is shown very clearly in the anonymous eighth-century Irish poem 'The Cry of the Deer', better known in English as 'St Patrick's Breastplate'. In the metrical version most familiar to us now, the relevant verse runs:

I bind unto myself today
     The virtues of the star-lit heaven,
The glorious sun's life-giving ray,
     The whiteness of the moon at even,
The flashing of the lightning free,
     The whirling wind's tempestuous shocks,
The stable earth, the deep salt sea,
     Around the old eternal rocks.

This is set within the wider context of a prayer for protection expressed in the next verse:

I bind unto myself today
     The power of God to hold and lead ...
The word of God to give me speech,
     His heavenly host to be my guard.

A journey across the causeway to Lindisfarne, along the Shannon to Clonmacnoise or following the cliff path to St Davids all still help us to recapture the delight of creation which was an essential part of the Irish-Celtic spiritual tradition. It also underlies a parallel emphasis in this tradition on love for one's native land. It is this which underpins the valid and healthy emphasis which has been recaptured in the rebirth of Celtic spirituality. The universality of the gospel and the authenticity of the local are held in tension.

FRUITS OF IRISH PILGRIMAGE

The lives of Brendan, Columba and Columbanus indicate the influence of Irish missionary monks well beyond the shores of their native isle. Celtic influence extends far from the shores of Britain and Ireland; we have already seen something of the wider spread of Celtic culture in all its forms. The pilgrim journeys of the early Irish saints left their mark in the evangelization of Europe and nowhere more clearly than in the Northumbrian monasteries of the seventh century, and in the mission to the rest of Britain which began in these Irish pilgrim powerhouses of prayer.

The Northumbrian tradition is significant for two particular reasons. First of all, we know more about this tradition, thanks to Bede and other contemporary chroniclers. Secondly, the Northumbrian monasteries, and the personalities associated with them, came to represent something quintessential in the Anglo-Saxon culture of the time. The key figure in the development of this tradition was Aidan. Oswald, the saintly King of Northumbria, had asked Iona for a bishop to be sent to proclaim the Christian gospel in his kingdom. The missionary bishop's ministry is described vividly by Bede:

> On Aidan's arrival, the king appointed the island of Lindisfarne to be his see at his own request. As the tide ebbs and flows, this place is surrounded by sea twice a day like an island, and twice a day the sand dries and joins it to the mainland. The king always listened humbly and readily to Aidan's advice and diligently set himself to establish and extend the Church of Christ throughout his kingdom.

Lindisfarne may seem an odd site to modern eyes for an ecclesiastical centre until we remember two considerations. First of all, we know of the love of the Irish missionaries for lonely sites well suited to solitude and prayer. Secondly, Aidan would have seen the importance of being close to the royal palace at Bamburgh. The wooden stakes across the sands to Holy Island mark the site of an ancient path that would have afforded Bishop Aidan ease of access to the royal presence. Aidan was known both as a wise counsellor and a man of humility. Such was the calibre of the monastery that he founded that for some three decades Lindisfarne would become the ecclesiastical centre of England, superseding even Canterbury in its preeminence. The manner of Aidan's ministry was after the Irish pattern: although Aidan was a bishop and he exercised an episcopal ministry, still he remained a monk. He would have been subjected to monastic vows and the rule of his abbot. The manner of Aidan's exercise of this ministry gave witness to his commitment to the life of holiness and to the Irish ascetic pilgrim tradition. As Bede observes,

> He never sought or craved for worldly possessions, and loved to give away to the poor who chanced to meet him whatever he received from kings or wealthy folk. Whether in town or country, he always travelled on foot unless compelled by necessity to ride ... His life is in marked contrast to the apathy of our own times, for all who walked with him, whether monks or lay-folk, were required to meditate or to learn the Psalms.

It was into this tradition that Cuthbert, perhaps the most revered of all the Northumbrian saints' was born. Cuthbert was an Englishman, probably born in about 634, but brought up in the Irish monastic tradition at Melrose. His master, as abbot of Melrose, was St Boisil (the origin of the modern St Boswell's) and Boisil schooled Cuthbert. Bede's *Life of Cuthbert* notes:

The community of Lindisfarne, he knew, was well adorned with holy monks, under whose example and teaching he might make good progress, but the reputation for sublime virtue enjoyed by Boisil, priest of Melrose, led him to enter there.

Cuthbert was to enjoy a similar if not enhanced reputation of sublime virtue. The remarkable *Lindisfarne Gospels*, completed probably in the year 698, eleven years after the saint's death, are a testimony to the honour in which his memory was held. Cuthbert was a true contemplative and the descriptions of his hermit-like existence on Inner Farne (where there is still a chapel dedicated to his memory) indicate his resolve, determination, and his holiness of life. He grew barley and made himself a virtually self-sufficient homestead there on the windswept volcanic isle in the North Sea. Despite this humble and pious life on Inner Farne, however, there are other signs that Cuthbert was clear about a proper episcopal dignity. Cuthbert both acted as a confessor and teacher within the monastery, at Melrose and at Lindisfarne. After the fashion of the Irish tradition, he too preached in villages and remote farmsteads, often going out on missionary journeys for anything from a week to a month in total. After the pattern of Aidan, even as a bishop he fed the hungry, cared for the poor, and comforted those who were in distress. He was noted particularly for a great variety of miracles and for his way with animals.

Cuthbert was also known for his ability to show humour and humanity but always to alert others to the foreboding dangers that beset the warlike and wild kingdom of Northumbria. One brief exchange from Bede's *Life* illustrates just this. Cuthbert foretells the death of King Egfrith:

'Brethren, I implore you, let us act prudently and be on our guard lest through taking neither care nor heed we be seduced by temptation.'

'For goodness sake,' they replied, 'let us enjoy ourselves today – it is Christmas, the birthday of our Lord Jesus Christ.'

'Very well, let us,' I replied. As things went on and we were enjoying our dinner, feeling convivial and telling stories, I broke in again to warn them to be earnest in prayer and vigils and to be ready against all temptation.

So Cuthbert went on with further fluctuations between mirth, enjoyment and dark prophecies of tragedy. The assembled company learned later that 'the king and all his bodyguards had been slaughtered by the enemy'. Although Bede's *Life* is undeniably hagiographic, still through the layers of hagiographic varnish, the humanity of Cuthbert communicates itself.

Alongside Cuthbert, other significant missionaries included Chad and Cedd, disciples of Aidan. Chad's memory has been preserved in Lichfield, as he is celebrated as missionary to the midlands of England. Bede notes that 'Chad established his episcopal seat in Lichfield (Lyccidfelth), where he also died and was buried, and where succeeding bishops of the province have their see to this day.'

Lichfield was for brief periods a province and thus the seat of an archbishop (656–8, 787–802). Evidence of Cedd's missionary work remains in two of the significant churches he founded, at Lastingham in Yorkshire (the present church is ancient but does not date back to the time of Cedd himself) and Bradwell. St Peter's Church at Bradwell is the seventh-century chancel of a church built on the site of the disused Roman fort of Othona, and indeed using the stone from the fort for the fabric of the church. Bradwell is reputed to have been the site of the conversion of the East Saxons through the baptism of their

King. Archaeologists and historians now date the church at Bradwell in the mid-point of Cedd's episcopacy, which was from 654 to 664. It is one of the most potent reminders of the strength and holiness of the Celtic mission to Britain.

THE CELTIC INHERITANCE

The widespread evidence of Celtic Christianity, from the Church of Cedd in Bradwell to the monastic ruins at Kildare, from Celtic crosses on the Cornish moors to similar relics in Iona or Britanny, and from Northumbrian memories of Aidan and Cuthbert to mainland European associations with St Brendan – all these bear eloquent testimony to the missionary zeal and the rich faith of our Irish and indeed Celtic forebears generally. Historical study and archaeological research have enabled us to appreciate and be fed by the beauty, the colour, and the breadth of Celtic patterns of Christian discipleship.

The work of Alexander Carmichael, during the last century, in collecting together the oral traditions of Celtic prayer has been equally enriching. His *Carmina Gadelica* are now widely known and have led to a rediscovery of this Christian literary and spiritual tradition and have even inspired others to write prayers in a similar style and spirit.

This recapturing of an inheritance that had been undervalued for so long helps us to redress a balance that is easily lost. A love and appreciation of creation, a feel for the landscape and place in which one is nurtured, and an embracing of the whole of life and offering it to God are clear themes in the Celtic Christian inheritance. The history of women saints and influential queens and female consorts reminds us too of the role of women alongside that of men. None of these is unique to the Celtic world although, as with all local traditions, the expression is certainly unparalleled. Similarly, the colouring of the tradition through the influence of pre-Christian culture is on one level a universal phenomenon, but in each locality particular.

As we learn anew to celebrate our Celtic inheritance, we do so for the enrichment we can receive and for the appreciation of the landscape and heritage that has helped mould us and which can further nurture our belief and worship. We celebrate that which is unique to our inheritance against the universal canvas of the Christian gospel. Celtic traditions contribute to that universality. To return to our guiding image, they influence the routes of our pilgrimage but they do not claim it for their own. As we move on to look at the wider Roman patterns of Christian theology and observance, we shall do so as all observers do, from the background of our own inheritance. As we do this, we shall see that the more universal pattern which extended throughout Europe is equally part of our own inheritance and has shaped us as Christian pilgrims in our own day.

Prayer

See that you be at peace among yourselves, my children,
and love one another,
follow the example of good men of old,
and God will comfort you and help you,
both in this world and in the world which is to come.

Prayer of St Columba, written on his deathbed for his
community in Iona, AD 597.

FOUR

ROADS FROM ROME

The mission sent by Gregory to the Anglo-Saxons begins with Augustine's preaching in Kent and is completed in Theodore's ordering of the English Church.

IN THE FOOTSTEPS OF AUGUSTINE

The tableau which forms the westernmost panel of the ceiling in Lambeth Palace Chapel in London depicts St Gregory the Great sending the young Italian monk Augustine to evangelize the pagan English. It hardly captures our contemporary understanding of pilgrimage, with its strong sense of a voluntary journey to a holy place. Instead, the neo-Byzantine figures, painted by Leonard Rosoman, show a stern and strong-minded Gregory sending a rather more submissive Augustine into the dark, heathen, Anglo-Saxon north. Augustine's long, thin fingers are extended in front of him, indicating a mood of both prayer and mission. His pilgrimage was enforced and by all accounts not always embraced with enthusiasm. He would have preferred to have lingered in the more cultured and warmer clime of Autun in Burgundy, than to have done business with the more primitive and perhaps unfriendly English.

The story of Augustine is both well known and yet also shrouded in the mists of time. Only the barest outline of the story is known to us. Augustine arrived in south-east England in the year 597. He disembarked (probably at Ebbsfleet) on what was then an actual island, Thanet. The low-lying and sometimes marshy land which now acts as the boundary to Thanet was in Augustine's day the Wantsum Channel. It was guarded at either end by the significant remains of the two Roman fortresses at Reculver and Richborough (evidence of the two remains, and fairly massively so at Richborough).

Augustine's mission in itself was a modest venture, aimed initially at the court of the Kentish King, Ethelbert. Ethelbert's court was based in Canterbury, the site of the Roman city of Durovernum. Despite our lack of detailed knowledge of Augustine's mission, some evidence does survive of both the place from which he departed, of his route (although this is not certain throughout) and of the city where he settled and eventually set up his episcopal see. It was from the spot where the basilica of St Gregorio Magna is now placed, in the year 576, that Augustine was sent out by his master, Pope Gregory the Great. Augustine was Italian by birth, and accounts suggest that he had been first a monk and then prior of the monastery of St Andrew, on the Celian Hill in Rome. As such, he was prefect of Gregory's own monastery, and he and his monks were thus under obedience to their pontifical master.

Augustine's route probably first took him and his party by sea to the southern French coast. Tradition suggests that they disembarked at the Iles de Lerins near Cannes and then made their way to Marseilles and up the Rhône valley, through Vienne and across via Autun to the Loire and Tours. Autun was the moment of Augustine's greatest hesitation. Bede describes his apprehension vividly:

Having undertaken this task in obedience to the Pope's command and progressed a short distance on their journey, they became afraid, and began to consider returning home. For they were appalled at the idea of going to a barbarous, fierce, and pagan nation, of whose very language they were ignorant.

Augustine was sent back to plead with Gregory that they might return to Rome. In reply, the Pope sent a letter of encouragement, the text of which Bede quotes. In that letter, Gregory refers to Augustine as 'Abbot', and it also seems clear that it was during the journey through Gaul that Augustine was ordained bishop. We do not know where Augustine's episcopal ordination occurred; Arles, Lyons and Autun are all possibilities. Gregory, as Bede notes, certainly commended the little missionary party to Etherius, the Archbishop of Arles. The diversion through Tours may now appear to us as more than a little eccentric; Tours is hardly on a direct route to Canterbury. There are two clear reasons, however, which might explain the diversion. First of all, it would have allowed the missionaries to stop and pray at the well-known shrine of St Martin of Tours, the missionary bishop. Martin was a popular missionary saint from the time of his death in 397 and throughout medieval times. Certainly, he had disciples in these islands and most notably in the person of St Ninian, who is said to have established his first church at Whithorn in Galloway, also in 397. The second reason for diverting through Tours is that there were close trading links between the Loire valley and Kent, and that a voyage would have been easily arranged.

On their arrival at Ebbsfleet, Augustine preached with vigour to King Ethelbert who reserved his judgement for the moment about the Christian faith. None the less, his confidence in Augustine was sufficient on this first meeting to give him a place of residence in his capital. Here, once again, we stumble upon resonances of St Martin, for Bede notes:

> On the east side of the city stood an old church, built in hon-our of St Martin during the Roman occupation of Britain, where [Ethelbert's Frankish wife Bertha] went to pray. Here they first assembled to sing the psalms, to pray, to say Mass, to preach and baptize, and until the King's own conversion to the Faith gave them greater freedom to preach and to build and restore churches everywhere.

St Martin's Church is one of three sites associated with Augustine, and mentioned in Bede's history, which are still vis-ible in Canterbury. Indeed, St Martin is probably the oldest parish church in England, having been in continuous use since the sixth century and dating back, according to Bede's account, to Roman times.

We can feel a further palpable link with the Augustinian mis-sion through the other sites which are mentioned by Bede:

> Having been granted his episcopal see in the royal capital, as already recorded, Augustine proceeded with the King's help to repair a church which he was informed had been built long ago by Roman Christians. This he hallowed in the name of our Saviour, God and Lord Jesus Christ, and established there a dwelling for himself and his successors.

It was this church that was to become the Cathedral Church of Christ in Canterbury and recently a further link in this history was established archaeologically. When in 1993 the nave paving was being replaced, the foundations of a Saxon church were discovered, offering us a glimpse of almost continuous worship on this site since the times of Roman Christianity in

Britain. What is now known as St Augustine's Abbey in Canterbury was also founded by the missionary from Rome in AD 598. Monastic building continued under Augustine's successors and the abbey was dedicated to Ss Peter and Paul in 613. Dunstan, Archbishop of Canterbury from 959 to 988, rebuilt and enlarged the church and added the name of Augustine to the dedication; thereafter it was known as St Augustine's Abbey. Augustine himself was buried in the north portico of the original church.

This remarkable evidence still extant in Canterbury, at St Martin's, St Augustine's Abbey and at the Cathedral, is powerful testimony both to the significance that Augustine's mission gained in later centuries, and to the clear-sightedness of Gregory the Great's missionary initiative. The Christian faith would now once again advance into what had been the farthest north-western outpost of the Roman Empire. A see was established at Canterbury at some point between Augustine's arrival in 597 and his death in about 604; established there, too, was both a monastery and a cathedral. It is impossible to make clear distinctions at this point between the role of monasteries and of cathedrals. This further warns us against making facile distinctions between the pattern of Celtic and Roman mission at this early stage. Canterbury became an urban episcopal centre. Further developments of a similar nature soon followed in Rochester (604) and in London (*c.* 604). (There had been bishops in London during Roman times.) But in Canterbury there remained also a community of missionary monks; the patterns established in rural communities by the Irish monks, where the abbot was also bishop, are not entirely contrasting.

Gregory the Great was keen that this symbiosis between monastery and cathedral should continue. Bede notes both in his *History* and in his *Life of Cuthbert* how Gregory had encouraged Augustine to live with his clergy.

You, brother, have been brought up in the monastic rule. Now that the faith has been brought to the English you must not start living apart from your clergy.

The English mission was first and foremost a Gregorian mission and the Pope's influence upon it was profound. In Gregory's initiative, something of both the Roman *imperium* and of the universality of Catholic Christianity in Europe was spread to the shores of these islands. Gregory was clear about the apostolic role of the see of Peter and of the pastoral and evangelical implications of the gospel. Also central to that mission was the life of prayer to which Gregory had originally been called – he had been snatched from a world of contemplation to the papal throne.

PAX ROMANA

Although the analogy ought not to be pressed, Britain, after the ending of the fourth century, assumed something of the feeling of the British Empire after the departure of the Raj. This was the world to which Ninian came; Whithorn was just over the wall from the decaying Roman Empire. The fortifications built by Hadrian on the Solway Firth would still have been visible. Even two centuries on, during his pontificate from 590 to 604, Gregory inherited some similar resonances. Rome was the city of St Peter and St Paul and, interestingly enough, the monastery in Canterbury founded by Augustine received that same dedication. Rome also remained the imperial city. As the son of a senator, Gregory himself had previously exercised public office in Rome, and as the Roman Pontiff was called once again to be a leader and an organizer within the Church. Gregory was aware of his position and that of the imperial centre in which he lived; elements of the Pax Romana lived on both in Church and state.

It is within this context that one must place the Gregorian mission to England, and indeed its later legacy. The missionaries who set out for England set out on one of the numerous 'roads from Rome'. Even in contemporary Italy the hub-like nature of Rome is clear as one makes one's way around the Grand Raccordo Annulare, Rome's orbital motorway. One great highway after another intersects – the Via Appia, the Via Aurelia, the Via Salaria and numerous other radial routes leaving the old imperial centre like spokes within a wheel. It was easy and indeed logical to see the network of roads across Europe and beyond as arteries within a missionary network. This network kept local churches in touch with each other and linked them to the see of Rome, presided over by the Roman Pontiff, who Gregory memorably described as the 'servant of the servants of God'. Such a pattern of jurisdiction and of pastoral care lay at the heart of Gregory's missionary impulse. He had a clear sense of responsibility for the health and well-being of all the Western churches. Indeed, it was this sense of pastoral care and responsibility that made Gregory one of the greatest of the medieval popes and one of those whose ministry and wisdom led to the enhanced power and dignity of the Papacy.

Gregory set out these ideals in his book on *Pastoral Care*. The character of the bishop, for Gregory, simply focused the attributes required by the gospel of all Christians. So he wrote: 'No art can be taught unless it is first learned by intense meditation; but the care of souls is of all arts the greatest; so you may judge the temerity of those who assume the office without preparation.' The bishop was to be a minister not a master. This pattern stood alongside his concern to pass on the wisdom of the Fathers, through his numerous writings, homilies and commentaries, to those who had stood outside the gospel.

The various migrations which were later styled the 'barbarian invasions' had left their mark on mainland Europe. His desire to preach the gospel to such people stood in parallel to his initiative with the Anglo-Saxons. The mission to the English, then, was thoroughly Gregorian and as such reflected his sensitivities and most notably his concern for pastoring the flock. It was to be comprehensive geographically, and in that sense the later development of the parish system in England by Archbishop Theodore of Tarsus was an extension and deepening of the Gregorian mission.

Gregory was clear about the authority which he had committed to Augustine. First of all, he had sent to him the *pallium*, a circular band of woollen material with two hanging strips and six dark purple crosses. The *pallium* signifies the authority of the Bishop of Rome and thus also the participation of other bishops in that authority. It symbolized the fact that the missionary road which Augustine was to travel was a road from Rome and it marked out the bishop's jurisdiction and place within the universal Church. Alongside sending Augustine this potent symbol of authority and pastoral care, Gregory made clear the ways in which the roads from Rome would be further extended into the urban centres of the Britannic islands:

> You are to consecrate twelve bishops in different places, who will be subject to your jurisdiction: the bishop of the city of London will thenceforward be consecrated by his own synod, and will receive the honour of the *pallium* from this apostolic see which, by divine decree, we at present occupy. We wish you also to send a bishop of your own choice to the city of York ...

Bede recounts Gregory's instructions with regard to the British bishops, those bishops indigenous to the islands before the arrival of the Gregorian missionaries. Gregory makes it clear that Augustine has no authority over the bishops of Gaul and notes that from earliest times the Bishop of Arles has received the *pallium*; Britain, however, is a different matter:

> All the bishops of Britain ... we commit to your charge. Use your authority to instruct the unlearned, to strengthen the weak, and correct the misguided.

Both here and elsewhere in Bede's account and, of course, in his *Pastoral Care*, Gregory expounds the mode of exercise of authority: the bishop is to live alongside his clergy; he is with them to support, nurture and presumably where necessary admonish them. Bishops, monks and all Christian people are called to live after the manner of the apostolic church:

> The whole company of believers was united in heart and soul. Not one of them claimed any of his possessions as his own; everything was held in common. With great power the apostles bore witness to the resurrection of the Lord Jesus, and all were held in high esteem. (Acts 4:32–33)

As Gregory observes, 'to those who live as a community there should be no need for us to mention allocating portions, exercising hospitality, and showing mercy'.

Augustine does not appear to have had within his bloodstream the same generosity in exercising authority nor the warmth exhibited by Gregory. His encounter with the British bishops makes this crystal clear. Undoubtedly the British (in this case, effectively Welsh) bishops will have been on the defensive. Augustine's party were seen as 'incomers' by indigenous Christians who saw their own patterns as authentic and well established. Bede shows that the dating of Easter was a substantive issue but alludes also to 'certain other of their customs' which were 'at variance with the universal practice of the Church'. The picture painted is of stubborn and almost bucolic prelates who are partially won over by Augustine's ability to perform a miracle by healing a blind man. This mollified them, but still they begged leave to consult further with their people on issues of ancient and local custom. This they were allowed.

At a second conference with Augustine, they sought a sign from a local hermit on how to know whether to compromise on their local customs. The hermit identified the sign as relating to Augustine's measure of humility. The means of assessing this was simple enough:

> If he rises courteously as you approach, rest assured that he is the servant of Christ and do as he asks ... if he ignores you and does not rise, then, since you are in the majority, do not comply with his demands.

The *dénouement* augurs ill for Augustine's diplomatic skills; he remained firmly seated. Even Bede's basic sympathy with the Roman cause is stretched to its limits. He makes no attempt to soften the blow. The Welsh are angry and flatly refuse to adjust their practice on the keeping of Easter and the administering of baptism. Augustine's response remains unbending and combative:

> ... if they refused to accept peace with fellow-Christians, they would be forced to accept war at the hands of enemies; and if they refused to preach to the English the way of life, they would eventually suffer at their hands the penalty of death.

Almost certainly this sorry tale stands at the heart of the negative contrasts now often made between the Roman and Celtic roots of Christianity in Britain and Ireland. An authentic local observance is contrasted with an exterior imposed authority; a blind and unthinking centralism is placed against a mature and long-founded autonomy; a juridical and cold demand is the response to a Christian community that has a clear pastoral heart. However, even a cursory glance at the story as told by Bede argues against such a simplistic dichotomy. The British are stubborn as well as intuitive. Augustine does demonstrate a care for the pastoral in the healing narrative despite his later crass insensitivity. Bede's account has all the elements of biased sources and incompleteness about it. None the less, Augustine's attitude can hardly be condoned.

Why did Augustine act as he did? We can only hazard a guess. Gregory was a good administrator. Almost certainly on such a mission, he would have wished to nominate someone with a similarly clear mind and sense of purpose. Augustine certainly seems to have had all these qualities. It appears, however, that Gregory's qualities of subtlety and perception may have passed him by. Indeed, it may also be the case that the tension in Gregory between the contemplative and the active was less developed in Augustine, in whom the rigours of the missionary administrator overcame some of the reflectiveness of the contemplative. The result was that even where different traditions overlapped and agreed, Augustine seemed unable to take both parties on a road to reconciliation.

An understanding of Gregory's background and qualities, together with a notion of what he intended Augustine to achieve can teach us much. Gregory's broad vision of a universal Church shaped by the resonances of the erstwhile Pax Romana would, if handled with care, not have required wholesale conflict with local traditions – *'things should not be loved for the sake of places but places for the sake of good things'*. Gregory exhorts a cherishing of the best local traditions. But alongside this, the local traditions are themselves grounded in, or manifestations of a wider common tradition from which all issued and through which all were shaped. The Irish, British, Gallican, Roman and Mozarabic – each was a scion of the broadest stream of European Christianity. Until the fall of Rome, indeed, such a common tradition was not confined to the West in contradistinction to the Byzantine East. The roads from Rome spoke of a true universality which at its best allowed the local communities to flourish with their own distinctiveness. If these roads were to bring the life blood of a universal Church then they must be extended outwards and the network of dioceses prospered.

UNTRODDEN ROADS?

The existence of Christian communities before both the Roman and Irish missions to Britain has been a recurring echo in these pages. The martyrdom of St Alban is perhaps the earliest and clearest evidence of Christian observance. The account of Augustine's meeting with the British bishops and the presence of bishops in London before the Gregorian mission all add to this picture. The Christian communities who worshipped at St Martin's, Canterbury and at the Church of the Saviour in that city are further signs of the gospel having been preached in Roman times. St Patrick is but one more witness.

In our earlier reflections upon Martin of Tours, the mission of St Ninian also came to light. Ninian is thought to have been born in Cumbria and then educated in Rome. Once again, our principal source of information on Ninian is Bede:

The southern Picts ... accepted the true Faith through the preaching of Bishop Ninian, a most reverend and holy man of British race, who had been regularly instructed in the mysteries of the Christian Faith in Rome. Ninian's own episcopal see, named after St Martin and famous for its stately Church ... belongs to the province of Bernicia and is commonly known as *Candida Casa,* the White House (Whithorn) because he built the church of stone, which was unusual among Britons.

Whether the church was itself dedicated to St Martin we cannot now be certain, but all accounts suggest that he was himself a disciple of the French soldier-missionary. Relics of St Martin have been found at Whithorn which bear striking parallels to similar archaeological finds discovered at St Martin's Church in Canterbury. Also a number of inscribed stones with the familiar Celtic patterns were discovered at Whithorn which can still be viewed there; these remains confirm the existence of a monastery nearby. Both the memory of Ninian and of other early British communities of Christians remind us that the missionary roads followed from the sixth century onwards were not untrodden. It is difficult, however, to trace any clear patterns or to know whether broader networks then existed.

With the advent of the Gregorian mission, a more systematic treading of the missionary roads began. Augustine consecrated the priest Laurentius, who had accompanied him on the original mission, as his successor. Bede notes that this followed the pattern of St Peter himself, who consecrated Clement as his successor. These details are, of course, now lost in the dim mists of antiquity, but Bede's reference has a broader significance; it was included to indicate both precedence and universality. Rome showed the historical pattern, and Rome was the source of authority. Bede quotes the epitaph said to have been inscribed on Augustine's tomb and which now, apart from

Bede's reference, is lost to us. In the epitaph, the universal and the local, the divine and the contingent are perfectly balanced:

> Here rests the Lord Augustine, first Archbishop of Canterbury, who, having been sent here by blessed Gregory, Pontiff of the City of Rome, and supported by God with miracles, guided King Ethelbert and his people from the worship of idols to the Faith of Christ. He ended the days of his duty in peace, and died on the twenty-sixth day of May in the above King's reign.

Laurentius, who succeeded Augustine, had been a key member of Augustine's party. He had been sent back to Rome to report progress. This report prompted Gregory to send Mellitus, in 601, to join Augustine. Mellitus' charge from Gregory again showed the subtlety of the Pope's mind. The original orders from Gregory had detailed Mellitus systematically to destroy pagan altars and images. In the event, however, the Pontiff had a radical change of mind, due almost certainly to his realization of the importance of an apologetic which took account of local loyalties and customs:

> ... the temples of the idols among [the English] people should on no account be destroyed. The idols are to be destroyed, but the temples themselves are to be aspersed with holy water, altars set up in them, and relics deposited there. For if these temples are well-built, they must be purified from the worship of demons and dedicated to the service of the true God.

Gregory goes further still, allowing the sacrificing of oxen to continue and indeed allowing the old feast days still to be kept. Other solemnities are to be substituted on these same days and the animals may be sacrificed for food to the praise of God. He reflects: 'If the people are allowed some worldly pleasures in this way, they will more readily come to desire the joys of the spirit.' Gregory asks Mellitus to inform Augustine of this policy, a policy whose implications may not be that far removed from those exercised by the Irish monks in relation to paganism in that land. Mellitus proved to be a faithful and even courageous missionary and pastor.

The other most famous companion of Mellitus in the second missionary party of 601, Paulinus, was less courageous. Paulinus preached the gospel to King Edwin of Northumbria and baptized his daughters. Paulinus later baptized the King. Tragedy struck, however, some six years later, when Edwin was killed in battle; Paulinus did not stay around to confess the faith amongst the pagan victors. Bede gives it as positive a gloss as possible: 'As a result of this disaster, the affairs of the Northumbrians were in such disorder that flight offered the sole hope of safety.'

Despite his lack of courage, Paulinus was a vigorous and effective missionary bishop. He travelled both the trodden and untrodden missionary paths of the Anglo-Saxon kingdoms, and memories and traditions of Paulinus' missionary journeying have left their mark widely. In Northumbria, alongside the royal household, Paulinus is said to have baptized hundreds in the River Glen, next to the royal palace at Ad Gefrin, now Yeavering in Northumberland. Similarly, the holy well and accompanying pool at Holystone near Rothbury, also in Northumberland, is another site where Paulinus baptized. Paulinus preached in Lindesey and in the city of Lincoln, too, where '... he also built a stone church of fine workmanship, which today, either through neglect or enemy damage, has lost its roof, although the walls are still standing'. In the 1970s, the site beneath the demolished nineteenth-century church of St Paul in Lincoln was excavated and, beneath the foundations of a medieval church, there was evidence of a much earlier church which may well have been that founded by Paulinus.

Although Paulinus' flight from Northumbria, and thus from his see at York, meant the end of the Roman mission in the north at that point, none the less we have seen something of the vigour and systematic mission which he represented. He was a man of some subtlety and perception. His return to Kent and to the see of Rochester led to the further consolidation of the Gregorian mission in the south-east. Paulinus' mission particularly illustrates the tendency of the Roman missionaries to establish urban sees in those Roman towns that showed some continuity of habitation – Canterbury, Rochester, London and York are the obvious examples. It was not so much then, that the roads that the Gregorian missionaries travelled were previously untrodden. Instead, they established those missionary paths as extensions of the original apostolic journey from Rome and as the beginning of a network of mission that would cover the entire land.

FROM ROADS INTO LANES

Pilgrimage, in a variety of forms, was an essential part of the spreading of the gospel in early medieval times. We have already heard of the pilgrimages of kings and princes to Rome and of Wilfrid and earlier still Ninian journeying to the eternal city. The pilgrimages of Augustine, Paulinus and others in the opposite direction brought Gregory's apostolic mission to these shores. A still more remarkable pilgrimage, by one who shared so much of Gregory's pastoral vision, put the final piece into the jigsaw of the Roman mission at this stage. Theodore of Tarsus was a sixty-seven-year-old monk from Cilicia in Asia Minor when he became Archbishop of Canterbury. He remained

Archbishop for twenty-one years and was effectively the initiator of the diocesan and parochial system which continues to this day.

Theodore's understanding of the work of the bishop and of the pattern of mission was utterly in the mould of Gregory.[1] Although he had not explicitly argued for small dioceses, the pattern that he envisaged for England implied as much. This was precisely the pattern that Theodore would develop during his archiepiscopate.

It would be wrong to read too great a degree of sophistication into the parochial/diocesan system at this point – there was no clearly defined system. Diocese and parish might be used for the same ecclesiastical units in different parts of Europe.[2] Nevertheless, from the time of St Martin of Tours onwards, the establishing of country churches offered the opportunity of developing a parish system as we would now understand it, within a wider diocesan unit.

The country churches established by Martin and others corresponded to the minsters which we have already encountered within Britain and Ireland at this time. Some of these minsters would have been straightforward monasteries, and others would have brought together groups of secular clergy leading a semi-community life. Some covered enormous areas and included a number of villages within their region or province. Historians have pointed out that village churches as we would now recognize them were fairly rare in the early Middle Ages.[3] The pattern just described has, of course, very strong resonances with the Irish pattern set out in the previous chapter. It was here that Theodore's genius was most creative and innovative. Effectively he was able, through his Eastern experience, to take the Irish traditions and blend them with the Roman patterns in a way that used the best of each and which meant that he remained loyal to his masters.

The key gathering which allowed the development of the new dioceses and an incipient parish system was the Synod of Hertford, convened by Theodore in the year 672. On his arrival in Canterbury, Theodore was faced with a church split into at the very most five dioceses. Some five years later he convened the Synod of Hertford and he moved with care.

Bede sets out the ten canons of the Synod, all of which appear to have been agreed by common consent, except for the ninth:

It was generally discussed, 'That more bishops shall be consecrated as the number of the faithful increases'. But we have announced no decision in the matter for the present.

Despite this, Theodore took his opportunities as they presented themselves and divided dioceses, including Wilfrid's see of Northumbria, while Wilfrid was in exile. A further sign of Theodore's accommodation of the Irish and Roman patterns was that whilst the sees were attached to urban centres with a long history of habitation, nevertheless, he also took account of political, regional and tribal divisions. East Anglia, for example, was divided into Norfolk and Suffolk with sees based at Elmham and either Dunwich or (more likely) Felixstowe, a geographical division that would disappear after the conquest and wait for more than eight hundred years before it was revived.

Both Theodore's methodical approach and his patience paid off. The canons of the Synod of Hertford still set a well-ordered pattern for the future. Clergy were effectively to be licensed to their bishop and not to wander freely offering an itinerant ministry; synods should be held twice a year; no bishops should claim precedence over another out of ambition; no bishop shall interfere in any way with monasteries dedicated to God. The division of sees offered a more effective pastoral care after the Gregorian model. Bede makes one further crucial point: 'Theodore was the first archbishop whom the entire Church of the English obeyed.'

FREEDOM AND ORDER

Theodore completed what Gregory and the Augustinian mission had begun. The apostolic mission which made its mark upon England over the century following Augustine's arrival placed a clear network of dioceses through which the entire nation might receive the gospel. But Theodore did not simply complete the work started by Augustine and Paulinus and their associates. His genius was to receive from the different missionary strands their strengths and their most attractive features. The freedom and flexibility of the Irish pattern of missionary monasteries continued. The order offered by the radiating missionary roads from Rome offered a pattern to establish a network of parishes and dioceses throughout the land. Flexibility meant that both the urban and the rural communities would receive true pastoral care. Order meant that dioceses would respect each other and would offer a model for communion and collegiality from which we are still able to learn at the present day. Tracing back the missionary roads to Rome offered a model of primacy rooted in the humility of Gregory's model of pastoral care, where the most honoured title, even of the Roman Pontiff, was 'servant of the servants of God'.

The achievement of this century was not arrived at without anguish nor without conflict. We have seen some of the vicissitudes through which the embryonic English church had already passed. The vagaries of politics and the rise and fall of kings left their marks. Power and politics were present also in the Church; when this was combined with a passion for the gospel and for unity with the Roman See further conflicts were inevitable. The controversy over the date of Easter, other underlying disagreements, and the presence of personalities like that of Wilfrid made the Synod of Whitby a necessity if a united mission was to be offered to the people of Anglo-Saxon kingdoms. That is the next episode in our unfolding story.

None the less, the ancient holy sites and indeed the cathedrals which still dominate our skyline testify to the effectiveness of the Irish and Roman missionary initiatives. They remind us powerfully of Columba and Aidan, of Augustine and Paulinus, of Gregory the Great and Theodore of Tarsus. They focus the mission of the seventh century, a mission of a European Church in its richness, its universality and its variety.

Prayer

Almighty and everlasting God,
the brightness of faithful souls,
who brought the nations to your light
and made known to them him who is the true light,
and the bright morning star:
Fill the world, we pray, with your glory,
and show yourself by the radiance of your light to all nations;
through Jesus Christ our Lord. Amen.

From the Gregorian Sacramentary

FIVE

GROWING TOGETHER

The two traditions of the Irish monasteries and the Roman missionaries encounter each other and from them issues a rich synthesis which becomes part of a European tradition.

THE BAY OF THE BEACON

She desired to forsake her country and all that she ever had, and go into France, there to lead a pilgrim's and exile's life for our Lord's sake.

In the event, these plans outlined by Bede, summarizing St Hilda's desire to become a pilgrim for God, were never realized. Instead, on her way to Gaul, she sojourned for twelve months in East Anglia and was then persuaded back to Northumbria by Aidan. Aidan installed her a year later as abbess at Hartlepool, where she remained for eight years. Then, in 657, King Oswy of Northumbria granted Hilda a property of ten hides at Whitby, then known as Streanaeshalch or the Bay of the Beacon. In that same year, Hilda founded the new abbey at Whitby, which some six years later would be the venue for the famous Synod of 663–4, when representatives of the Celtic and Roman traditions met under the presidency of King Oswy.

The ruins of Hilda's great double monastery are still commanding and Whitby's remarkable position gives to the Abbey an even greater prominence. Celtic Christianity's stress on nature is suitably remembered here. The proximity of the sea and of panoramic views, together with the small fishing fleet which still plies from the harbour, reminds us of the dependence of humanity upon God's creation, for food and for safety. Doubtless this dramatic site inspired the poet and cowherd Caedmon to reflect upon creation and Creator. Both the views from the small Victorian resort north of the Esk and the climb up the 190 steps to the abbey suggest a great strength and witness represented in the site of the abbey. It was a beacon and a fortress standing defiant against the wiles of the devil and the strong tempests of an often unfriendly world.

Whitby was a double monastery. As such it bore witness to a wider European culture and Christian life, which was already a reality in the seventh century. For this tradition of double monasteries had entered these islands via the Church in Gaul. Double monasteries in Gaul traced their origins to women (often of noble birth) responding to the missionary initiatives of the great Irish monk Columbanus. Hilda stood in this tradition of aristocratic women – she was related to the royal households of both Northumbria and East Anglia. Men's communities grew up alongside in order to assist in practical and administrative tasks which women might not be able to accomplish alone; they would also, of course, celebrate the Eucharist and offer the other priestly ministrations which were not open to the sisters.

Hilda herself illustrates an interesting confluence of traditions. Baptized and nurtured in her faith by the Roman missionary Paulinus, she learned the monastic customs of the Irish Celtic tradition through her friendship with Aidan. She was an impressive exemplar of the Anglo-Saxon tradition of able women attaining to great authority and influence. Bede notes that five men from her monastery at Whitby became bishops – Bosa, Aetla, Oftfor, John, and Wilfrid. Hilda was formidable both in her holiness and in her vision and leadership within the abbey. Bede writes:

> She ... taught the observance of righteousness, mercy, purity, and other virtues, but especially of peace and charity ... Those under her direction were required to make a thorough study of the Scriptures and occupy themselves in good works, to such good effect that many were found fitted for Holy Orders and the service of God's altar.

It was a measure of Hilda's achievement that Whitby was chosen as the venue for the great Synod in 663–4. This relatively new monastery would serve as the place of residence for two kings, a number of bishops, an abbot, and all their retinues. The abbey, in its exposed cliff top location, would truly become a beacon on the bay, and indeed a beacon within the Anglo-Saxon Church. Although Hilda would support the Celtic lobby during the Synod, we have already seen how her own experience and background spilt out well beyond the prescribed confines of one tradition.

Hilda's enthusiasm for learning was demonstrated by her commitment to the establishment of libraries and the thorough education of clergy in Latin literature and language. Recent excavations of Whitby abbey have led to the discovery of book covers and styluses which indicate the existence of both a library and a scriptorium. These same excavations have revealed the existence of two churches, a pattern followed by the later Gilbertine order of double monasteries. The cells each had two rooms and a hearth and were grouped in the Celtic fashion; there was extensive accommodation for guests. All this indicates how much of a 'power house' Whitby was under Hilda's leadership and tutelage.[1]

After her death, a cult began almost immediately, and she who had seen her religious offering in the image of a pilgrimage became the focus of pilgrimage herself. Bede tells us how Hilda's mother had seen in a dream the remarkable future for which her daughter was destined:

> In this dream she fancied that [her husband] was suddenly taken away, and although she searched everywhere, she could find no trace of him. When all her efforts had failed, she discovered a most valuable jewel under her garments; and as she looked closely, it emitted such a brilliant light that all Britain was lit by its splendour. This dream was fulfilled in her daughter, whose life afforded a shining example not only to herself but to all who wished to live a good life.

Hilda's influence and contribution to the life of the seventh-century church is a further indicator of the essential part played during this missionary period by religious. Mission, learning, and prayer were all of a piece and they were not dissociated from the secular. Hilda's own origins in two royal houses and indeed her continued commerce with bishops and kings is resonant with the heartbeat of the time. Cathedrals would draw their strength from the monastic life, and therefore the patterns of worship and holy life established in those places influenced the development of mission. Those who would gather in 663–4 at the Synod of Whitby were sharply aware of this. None would see it more clearly than Hilda herself and indeed Wilfrid, who was to be so formative in setting the pattern for the discussions which took place. Standing on the cliffs north of the River Esk today still gives one a dramatic view of the place where the missionary traditions in England had begun to grow together.

OSWY VOTES FOR ROME

The controversy which led to the convening of the Synod of Whitby was mirrored, remarkably enough, within the royal household of Northumbria itself. The traditions that had formed Oswy, the King, had been those of Irish monasticism and mission; Eanfleda, his Queen, however, came from the Roman observance. The royal couple therefore rarely found themselves celebrating Easter at the same time, even within the same household. This difference in custom was understandably reflected in wider culture and would eventually have its effects politically as well as ecclesiastically. Although this may appear to be a pedantic theological argument, rooted in astronomical technicalities, temperatures ran high.

Bede talks of this dispute as a 'great and recurring controversy' and he is clear that the 'Irish observance of Easter was contrary to that of the universal Church'. So, despite his admiration for Aidan and Cuthbert, Bede is convicted of the overriding significance of the unity of God's Church. The degree of division on this issue is often exaggerated. Even in Ireland, in the south the Roman observance was accepted, as it was, of course, by the Gregorian mission to England and its inheritors. In Iona, however, and within that group of churches associated with it, this different observance survived. Indeed, the decision of Whitby did not settle it for all, and Bishop Colman of Lindisfarne returned to a voluntary exile in the north of Ireland so that he might remain loyal to his tradition.

What exactly was the Easter debate? It pivoted around two separate points of controversy. The first issued from the question of Easter's relationship to the dating of the Jewish Passover, and the second was an astronomical question relating to cycles of years based on lunar months. But neither of these technical questions need detain us here, for it was a more profound

matter that lay at the heart of the debate. If Easter is the celebration of the Lord's resurrection then it is arguably the central
feast of the Christian calendar. If the local churches could not
agree about the dating of this main Christian feast, there
seemed little hope in achieving agreement upon other more
complex theological matters.

The decision to call a Synod was almost certainly due to the
pressure of Alfrith, the son of Oswy and the King of part of
Deira. Alfrith had been converted to the Roman observance
and through this controversy saw the possibility of increasing
his power over against that of his father. In pressing for this
council, however, Alfrith underestimated the political shrewd-
ness of Oswy. Oswy is not portrayed by Bede as someone who
was prone to religious fanaticism, so his eventual change of
mind on the matter of the Irish and Roman observances should
not be seen as too drastic. He was clear about the need for political unity and stability. The fact that he and his wife could not
celebrate Easter together acted as a potent reminder of the
practical effects of the divergences of ecclesiastical traditions.

Oswy's son had changed his mind due to the influence of
Wilfrid, whose journeyings in Gaul and to Rome had pressed
home the imperative of there being a universal observance
within the Church on this and all matters of theology. In Eddius' *Life of Wilfrid*, the biographer has his master quoting the
Fathers of the Council of Nicaea in support of the Roman argument. Nicaea, in AD 325, had been the venue for the first ecumenical council of the early Church, called to settle questions
of the nature of Christ, and particularly to suppress the so-
called Arian heresy to which we referred in an earlier chapter.
That council had also been presided over by the secular ruler –
in this case the recently converted emperor, Constantine. In antiquity and in medieval times we should never underestimate
the significance of secular politics in the life of the Church, nor

conversely of the Christian religion in the life of the body politic. So, Oswy listened carefully to the arguments rehearsed, since he realized that political stability might be at stake. Following the conclusion of Wilfrid's defence, Eddius reports (my italics):

> At the end of Wilfrid's speech, Oswy asked them [the gathered clergy from both traditions], *with a smile on his face*, 'Tell me, which is greater in the Kingdom of Heaven, Columba or the apostle Peter?' [Bishop Colman had used Columba as his authority and Wilfrid had referred to the authority accorded to Peter in Matthew 16:18–19.] The response was resounding: then the whole synod with one voice and one accord cried: 'The Lord Himself settled this question when He declared'.

Then the reference to Matthew's Gospel is once again quoted in the account of Eddius. The King, in both versions, is more than content with this argument and in Bede's *History* concludes:

> Then, I tell you, Peter is the guardian of the gates of heaven, and I shall not contradict him. I shall obey his commands in everything to the best of my knowledge and ability; otherwise, when I come to the gates of heaven, there may be no one to open them, because he who holds the keys has turned away.

Oswy's political acumen and foresight are evident. In allowing the synod to come together and facilitate the exchange of scholarly opinions he effectively defused much of the potential conflict. The decision reached at the synod by the King did not simply mean a triumph for the Roman bishops – in this sense the King was shrewder than the prelates. Oswy knew that tribal feelings remained strong and that loyalty to indigenous traditions required a flexibility not shown by Wilfrid alongside his eloquent debating skills. Ultimately the solution allowed both traditions to grow together and offer something richer than might have been possible by adhering to one with rigidity. The model of the relationship of Christianity to culture is encouraging and is a model which has recurred to the credit of the gospel throughout the Christian era.

The essence of the debate for Wilfrid and others was nothing less than the universal nature of the Church and a recognition of the primacy of the Bishop of Rome. The controversy over Easter symbolized divisions in a most powerful way, but it by no means exhausted the points of disunity. Differing religious tonsures and the manner of chanting in monasteries were two more outward and visible signs of a more profound fragmentation. Of greater significance was the debate over the true exercise of episcopacy. How should monasteries and bishops relate to each other? Augustine had already faced this question and it would still be an issue in the time of Lanfranc and Anselm following the Norman conquest of England. The Irish tradition had effectively been monastic, and bishops had exercised their ministry in obedience to an abbot. The Roman tradition saw the bishop as exercising an authority with dignity and power both in Church and state; this was clearly the pattern in the Merovingian Church in Gaul. It was the pattern preferred by Wilfrid. The two models stood alongside each other in England, but they could not coexist in this way forever.

None the less, the ultimate *dénouement* did not turn out to be quite in the 'black-and-white' terms that Wilfrid styled the debate. Within only half a century or so after the Synod of Whitby, happy relations already existed between communities which might easily have preserved rancour on both the personal and corporate level. So for example, Lindisfarne, the ancient centre of the Irish-Celtic observance, and Wearmouth/Jarrow, the newer centre influenced by the Roman traditions of Benedict Biscop and Wilfrid, showed strong affection for each other. This is clear from the warmth expressed by Bede (who concluded his *History* in 731 at Jarrow) in the prologue to his *Life of Cuthbert*:

> To my holy and most blessed lord and father, Bishop Eadfrid, and to the whole congregation of monks serving God at Lindisfarne, Bede, your faithful servant, sends greeting ... On behalf of our congregation, beloved brethren and masters, I pray that the Almighty Lord may keep you secure in bliss. Amen.

Much of the credit for this remarkable growing together of traditions should redound to the leaders of the Church at that time. Cuthbert's holiness and the respect in which he was held is almost legendary; although his emotional roots were in the Irish tradition, he accepted the decision of Whitby. Theodore took both traditions and brought them together such that the local could remain and be respected for centuries to come. Practically, many of these local traditions were lost for a time due to the frequency and ferocity of the Viking invasions, but they were restored in the Benedictine monastic renewal of Dunstan in the tenth century. Furthermore, Theodore's imaginative and creative vision of a diocesan and parochial pattern combined elements from the two observances in a model of the episcopate which was superior to both the original Celtic and Roman. Such responses mirrored a generosity of response not always reflected in the career of Wilfrid, one of the most brilliant Christian leaders of this period, a period that Bede clearly looked back on as a golden age.

WILFRID'S ACHIEVEMENT

'If there were popularity stakes for the story of the Anglo-Saxon conversion to Christianity, they would not be won by Wilfrid.'² Undoubtedly this assessment is true. Even Bede's own account of Wilfrid, admiring as it is, fails to produce a fulsome appreciation of all aspects of the saint's life. Nevertheless, as with so much comment upon the two missions to these islands in the seventh century, the picture has been overdrawn, positions polarized and personalities caricatured.

There is no doubting Wilfrid's ability, his commitment and indeed his contribution to the seventh-century mission as a whole. Indeed, it is at times his rigour and clarity of mind that make him less attractive and indeed less effective in persuading others of the rightness of his approach. Wilfrid's commitment and rigour are focused sharply in his reply to Archbishop Dalfinus of Lyons' suggestion that he might stay in Gaul as a governor and marry the archbishop's niece. Once again it is the theme of pilgrimage that focuses Wilfrid's aspirations and sense of vocation:

> I have made my vows to the Lord and I shall keep them, leaving, like Abraham, my kinsfolk and my father's house to visit the Apostolic See, there to learn the laws of ecclesiastical discipline so that our nation may grow in the service of God ... If with God's help I am still alive, I promise to come back to see you.

Wilfrid certainly did journey on, and one might easily describe the rest of his life as a missionary pilgrimage. It is interesting that he sees his mission as including an element of edifying people such that 'the nation may grow in the service of God'. This was probably both a response to Archbishop Dalfinus' offer of a governorship in Gaul, and to his own youthful experience where he mixed with the court of Queen Eanfleda of Northumberland; through her encouragement, Wilfrid joined the monastic community on Lindisfarne during the time of Aidan. Wilfrid was restless at Lindisfarne and decided to make his way to Rome in the company of Benedict Biscop. It was during this journey that Wilfrid stayed on for a year at Lyons as the guest of the archbishop there.

The influence on Wilfrid of these early years on the mainland continent was profound. Here he would begin to appreciate more fully the significance of the traditions of Peter at Rome and gain a clear perception of the Church universal. Here, too, Wilfrid's understanding of both the role of the bishop and the nature of a diocese was formed. It was not simply a question of the size of the dioceses that Wilfrid learned in Gaul and in Italy, it was also a question of resources. For the size of a diocese was bound to affect the scale of a bishop's income. Church taxes assured the bishop of an income, and the larger the diocese, the more likely that that income could support the mission of local Christian communities and the building of minsters and cathedral churches. Wealth, splendour and dignity also allowed prelates to be compared with secular rulers and so to be offered an appropriate respect. This in itself would contribute to the effective ministry and presence of a bishop within his flock. Wilfrid's powerful mind and his potential for leadership developed in the wider context of Western Christendom, pushing his horizons beyond the local patterns of Irish monasticism of his native Northumbria.

Wilfrid returned home from his journeyings and Alfrith gave him the land at Ripon upon which he established his monastery. He was ordained priest in 663 and became the first abbot of Ripon. Following his estimable performance at the Synod of Whitby and the subsequent confirmation of the Roman way by

King Oswy, Wilfrid was sent to be ordained bishop in Gaul. Initially, there being no see vacant on his return, Wilfrid continued to lead the monastic community at Ripon. He built Ripon in the Roman style and introduced the Rule of St Benedict; in doing so he brought the Benedictine observance for the first time to Northumbria. In 669, Theodore gave him episcopal jurisdiction. With Oswy's support, he was made Bishop of York with pastoral care of the whole of Northumbria. During this period, Wilfrid was at the height of his powers and building went on apace not only at Ripon, but also at Hexham and York.

In 678, Theodore divided the diocese of Northumbria in two with the support of King Egfrith. Egfrith's motives were doubtless dubious and political, perhaps reflecting a sense of threat posed by the energetic, intelligent and striving Wilfrid. Theodore was merely pursuing his policy of smaller dioceses, a policy which also ran against the Gallican vein of Wilfrid's own thinking. His quickness of wit, irritation on having his 'kingdom' halved and his understanding as a canon lawyer, all drove him to Rome to pursue his case. The Pope, in true political and diplomatic style, affirmed both parties; the division of the diocese was confirmed whilst at the same time arguing for the correctness of Wilfrid's canonical position. On his return, Egfrith placed Wilfrid in solitary confinement and eventually sent him into exile.

Wilfrid's energies were now employed to take the gospel to the South Saxons. His landing on the south coast at Selsey is commemorated by the existence of a medieval chapel, now a little way inland. The chapel is that which was immortalized in Rudyard Kipling's 'Eddi's Service':

Eddi, priest of St Wilfrid
    In his chapel at Manhood End,
Ordered a midnight service
    For such as cared to attend.

But the Saxons were keeping Christmas,
    And the night was stormy as well,
Nobody came to the service,
    Though Eddi rang the bell ...

'Wicked weather for walking',
    Said Eddi of Manhood End.
'But I must go on with the service
    For such as care to attend.'

The romantic flavour of these lines should not conceal the zeal and energy which Wilfrid demonstrated in his new missionary journeys. These journeys, however, showed Wilfrid in less combative mood than before and also marked out powerfully his missionary methods as Gregorian in their approach. Columba and Columbanus, reflecting the tradition of Martin of Tours, had pursued a confrontational and dramatic approach to their missionary task. The accommodation which became central to the Gregorian mission, which attempted to use pagan sites and Christianize them, was not the way of some of the Irish missionaries. Wilfrid's attitudes to the precise teaching of Gregory on pagan temples and idols are not known, but what is clear is that it was more a matter of persuasion combined with a clearer instinctive sensitivity to the world in which the missionary worked than was the case with the patterns established by the soldier-saint, Martin of Tours. Bede describes Wilfrid's approach thus:

For when Wilfrid had first arrived in the province and found so much misery from famine, he taught the people to obtain food by fishing ... By this good turn the bishop won the hearts of all, and the people began to listen more readily to his teaching, hoping to obtain heavenly blessings through the ministry of one to whom they already owed these material benefits.

The later years of Wilfrid's life were as colourful as those we have already described. Returning to Northumbria, there followed further disputes, virtual house arrest and effective exile. Again Wilfrid made his plea to Rome and again he was vindicated. True peace did not break out until the year 705, at a synod convened on the River Nidd, where it was agreed that Wilfrid's monasteries at Ripon and Hexham should be restored, together with the Bishopric of Hexham. His life was now drawing near to its close. He died, Bede tells us, in a monastery in the region of Oundle, and was carried by the brethren to his first monastery at Ripon.

Wilfrid was a complex and in some ways flawed personality. Nevertheless, the remarkable nature of his achievement and his contribution to the growth of English Christianity is undeniable. Even accounting for his angularities, in Wilfrid there is again a confluence of the various traditions which gave birth to the gospel in England. Schooled in the Irish tradition, Wilfrid matured in the Roman patterns of mainland Europe. It was his very clarity of mind about the traditions that he inherited that so often made him both a tireless co-worker and also a fearless fighter for what he believed to be the truth. He was a man of pride, energy and determination but easily prone to rigidity and dominance; he was a courageous and sometimes contemptuous leader rather than a natural contemplative. Even here, however, there is room for qualification. In introducing

Benedictine spirituality and life to Northumbria, the legacy he left behind complemented the established patterns of the Irish monasteries. Furthermore, he never faltered in his own life of prayer. During his imprisonment Wilfrid did not desert his Lord:

> Wilfrid, whose faith was so great by now that he might well have been called the light of Britain, was to be locked up in a pitch-black dungeon and securely guarded ... His guardians, hearing him continually sing psalms, looked into the cell and found the darkness of the night turned into day. Thunderstruck themselves, they terrified others with the tale of his holiness.

Even allowing for Eddius' ever-present hagiographic gloss, Wilfrid's character still shines through. His sense of pilgrimage, his vision of a wider Europe, his encounter with the Rule of St Benedict and thus his grip upon the wider Church indicate a new leap forward in the mission to England. The roads from Rome meet the Irish patterns and begin to grow together. As they do so, they provide both the richness and the strength for the new missionary impulse to move outwards and offer nourishment to mainland Europe.

JOURNEYS OUTWARD AND INWARD

Wilfrid had journeyed out through Lyons to Rome with Benedict Biscop as his companion. In Bede's *Lives of the Abbots of Wearmouth and Jarrow*, reference is made to at least five journeys of Benedict to the eternal city. Throughout, the main stress in Bede's accounts of these journeys is one of the riches that were bestowed upon to the English Church through these pilgrim voyages. Benedict brought back books, relics of the apostles and martyrs, sacred pictures, and he introduced into his monastery 'the order of chanting and singing the psalms and conducting the liturgy according to the practice in force at Rome'. From France, Benedict brought masons to build a stone church in the Roman style, glaziers to glaze the windows of the church and sacred vessels and vestments. While undoubtedly the emphasis is on a movement towards Britain of continental custom and tradition, Benedict's stays in mainland Europe were sufficiently extended for us to assume that a real intercourse between traditions would have occurred.

Similar assumptions may be made about the various journeys made by Wilfrid to Rome, and particularly in relation to his three-year sojourn as the guest of Archbishop Dalfinus. For not only did Wilfrid delay in Lyons as Benedict Biscop travelled on to Rome, he also returned to Gaul and stayed there for three years before returning to found his first monastery at Ripon. In Lyons, Eddius tells us, Wilfrid received the Roman form of tonsure and he remained in Lyons and witnessed the violent death and so the martyrdom of Dalfinus. Remembering the rich confluence of traditions and the sophisticated intellectual blend of theologies that we have already encountered in Wilfrid, we can certainly be assured of the influence that the young monk will have had in southern Gaul. In that sense we can see Wilfrid's missionary impulse as being universal. This is confirmed by his missionary journey to Frisia during his exile from Northumbria in the time of Egfrith; Wigbert and Willibrord would build upon Wilfrid's Frisian mission some fifteen years later. Wigbert was clearly a less talented evangelist than Willibrord. Bede comments: '... his great efforts produced no results among his barbaric hearers'. Willibrord's mission was outstanding: '... consequently [Willibrord and his companions] converted many folk in a short while from idolatry to belief in Christ'. Two of his companions, differentiated only by the colour of their hair,

Hewald the Black and Hewald the White, suffered martyrdom during this mission.

These examples of evangelization and journeying indicate a strong outward missionary impulse within seventh and eighth century Anglo-Saxon Christianity. Part of this impulse doubtless owed its origins to the enthusiasms of Wilfrid and his disciples to establish widely the Roman observance of Easter. The richness and variety in these missionary journeys and in the personalities who led them suggest other stimuli, however, alongside the desire to spread Roman customs more widely. That tradition that has followed us throughout, the Irish pilgrimage for God, with its oblique missionary implications, is almost certainly there, too. Then finally, the impulse which found its origins in the Gregorian mission, and which traced its motivation to that remarkable blend of contemplative prayer and pastoral care and service seen in Gregory the Great himself, is also a likely influence upon the Anglo-Saxon tradition. Which of these may have been the most significant we cannot now decide. It is undeniable, however, that by the end of the seventh century, Anglo-Saxon Christianity had adopted an outward-looking missionary stance that is captured classically in the life of St Boniface and in his work in Germany.

Boniface was a West Saxon, from Devon, who spent almost the entire second half of his life as a missionary in northern Europe; he was born in 675 and died in 754. Boniface worked with the early rulers of the Frankish Carolingian dynasty which ruled in France from 751 to 987. In style, he followed the Gregorian pattern of persuasion rather than violence. Boniface also emulated Wilfrid in gathering to himself a strong team of co-workers, and in being influenced by his loyalty to the Papacy. Boniface was clear, however, of his own authority as an archbishop and metropolitan with responsibility in his own province. In this, once again, the universal and the local both

survived. The encounter between the Irish and Roman observances had led to a greater richness rather than a dull uniformity. Boniface's impact in Germany, based on his great
monastery at Fulda, was immense. He extended effective papal
authority in northern Europe, but he also helped establish the
distinctive style and tradition of the Carolingian bishops. Both
secular and ecclesiastical politics once again helped shape the
precise patterns of Boniface's missionary endeavours.

EUROPEAN CHRISTIANITY

In his seminal writings on the history of European culture,
Christopher Dawson has remarked upon the conversion of the
Barbarian migrants and of the subsequent complex interrelation which developed between Church and state with the extension of the Carolingian Empire. This, he argues, results in a
Carolingian understanding of Christianity as a force for social
unity. The Carolingian Empire becomes a society of Christian
people.[3] Hints of such a movement have already made themselves clear as we have seen the Irish and Roman traditions in-
teracting with each other in Britain in the eighth century and
leading to a wider missionary impulse. An even stronger resonance with Dawson's reflections is there in the impulse which
lay behind Gregory's missionary initiative which bore fruit in
the arrival of Augustine on the shores of Kent in 597.

The creative interplay between Gregory's missionary philosophy and the rich traditions represented in the Irish monasteries manifests itself time and again and in a variety of different
ways. It is there in the great achievement of Theodore. It is present in the remarkable writings of Bede, where loyalty to Rome
is combined with an unstinting admiration for the spiritual and
theological treasury represented by the Irish-Celtic monastic

tradition. It is there even in the more angular and sometimes over-incisive contribution of Wilfrid. It meant that the Synod of Whitby, for example, was not the triumph for the Roman supporters as it is so often crudely portrayed. Local traditions lived on. The tension between the local and the universal did not die, and it is seen very clearly, for example, in the impatience with which Archbishop Lanfranc confronted what he saw as bizarre and outlandish local customs.[4] As well as attempting to suppress the observance of the feasts of some particularly obscure local saints, Lanfranc imported new Benedictine monks from Bec in Normandy to the monastery in Canterbury. The indigenous English monks and the 'new imports' lived on beyond Lanfranc's time in undeniable hostility.

The increasing influence (well before Lanfranc's time) of the Rule of St Benedict in the early medieval period was undoubtedly a key contribution to the growth of a European Christian tradition. We have seen the significance of this in the life of Wilfrid. Boniface, too, was the product of the encounter between the Irish-Celtic and Benedictine monastic traditions. Bede and Cuthbert, both monks, also knew and valued the Rule of St Benedict. The encounters between these two traditions was to exercise a most profound influence upon the development of European culture. The Benedictine tradition, represented by Gregory the Great and thus by Augustine and his companions, has already been part of our story.

The pattern that is discovered in a careful reflection upon the twin roots of Christianity in Britain and Ireland is one of great complexity and profound beauty. The story is told in a great tapestry which is woven upon the canvas of Western Christianity. Upon that canvas are woven an enormous variety of different tableaux representing the local traditions. Even those local tableaux are a subtle interweaving between different local traditions. This has become clear as we have seen the unfolding missionary story that goes to and from these islands. This richness is the inheritance upon which we are able to draw as we seek anew in every generation to understand the implications of the gospel almost two thousand years after the death of Christ. The canvas of our civilization has now changed and developed, and the nature of that canvas will itself affect how we understand that which is now called out of us as disciples in our own time.

Prayer

> *Praise now the maker of the heavenly kingdom*
> *the power and purpose of our Creator,*
> *the deeds of the Father of glory.*
> *Let us sing how the eternal God,*
>   *author of all miracles,*
> *first created the heavens for the sons of men*
>   *as a roof to shelter them,*
> *and how their almighty Preserver gave them*
>   *the earth to live in.*
>
>   *Amen.*

Prayer written by Caedmon, poet and herdsman at the monastery at Whitby.

LIVING
TRADITION

SIX

THE LOCAL AND THE UNIVERSAL

Neither the human community nor the Church can live without both local freedom in tradition nor without respecting our inter-dependence across all communities.

South-west Wales, notably Pembrokeshire, has a character all of its own. In the earlier and arguably less sensitive decades of this century it was sometimes known as 'Little England Beyond Wales'. In essence, however, there could be no less appropriate label for this part of Wales, for the extreme south-west reaches of the country take us deep into the heart of the Celtic inheritance of our islands. The return of monks to Caldey Island off the coast near Tenby, earlier this century, is a potent reminder of the religious tradition which was firmly estab-lished in these parts already in the fifth century. The rugged and romantic coastline is strongly suggestive of a world where coracles (tiny fishing boats) abounded, transporting holy car-goes of missionaries to and fro over the Irish Sea. Some tradi-tions suggest that Patrick, the Briton who became patron of Ireland, was born in Wales.

It is the memory and inheritance of Dewi, however – better known outside the Principality as St David – that stands at the heart of this evocative and sacred peninsula in south-west Wales. The noble cathedral at St Davids and the ruins which surround it speak of a rich Christian heritage. David is the only Welsh saint to have been canonized by the Western Church. Whether his original monastery was at Menevia (St Davids) or not is now uncertain, but it is likely that he did set up a monastery at St Davids, possibly in the mid to late sixth century; dates for his death are variously given as 589 and 601. Sadly, little detail is known about his life. Indeed, the first life of Dewi was written by Rhygyvarch in about 1090. Rhygyvarch gives a vivid account of the strictly ascetic life in Dewi's monastery at Menevia. Physical labour stands at the centre of this life:

> They place the yoke upon their shoulders; they dip the ground unweariedly with mattocks and spades; they carry in their holy hands hoes and saws for cutting, and provide with their own efforts all the necessities of their own community. Possessions they scorn, the gifts of the wicked they reject, and riches they abhor. There is no bringing in of oxen to have the ploughing done, rather is every one both riches and ox unto himself and the brethren. The work completed, no complaint was heard: no conversation was held beyond that which was necessary, but each one performed the task enjoined with prayer and appropriate meditation.

After this work, there was time for study, before the evening bell was rung which called them to prayer.

It appears that Dewi came from Cardiganshire where he began his life as a monk. Having established his own monastery at Menevia, he later used this as the focus of a missionary movement which extended throughout Dyfed, the south-west corner of Wales. The influence of Dewi and his disciples was significant. Not only did they preserve their own religious traditions, but they acted as the focus of a Welsh cultural and linguistic tradition. It may be this that ultimately, from the twelfth century onwards, earned Dewi the honour of becoming the patron of Wales.

Theologically, the influence of Dewi and his community was also important. The Pelagian heresy, which we have encountered before, and which was opposed to the Augustinian (Augustine of Hippo) stress upon the primacy of God's grace, continued to thrive in parts of Dyfed. This heresy had been countered by the wider Church over the past two centuries. Dewi continued this work and led the opposition to Pelagianism.

This role is of particular significance as we begin to investigate and appreciate the interrelationship between the local and the universal. On one level, Dewi, a Romano-British monk who shared the inheritance of Patrick, is the prototype exemplar of local traditions within Christianity. Even more than the Irish monasteries set up by Columba and his inheritors on Iona and in north-east England, the British tradition was seen as out of step with the rest of the Church; this tradition received the strongest censure in Bede's *Ecclesiastical History*. In Bede's view, the British bishops were stubborn defendants of patterns of Christian life that failed to take account of the wider Western tradition. But Dewi's anti-Pelagianism shows this contrast to be too crude. In the early fifth century, Germanus of Auxerre had addressed a meeting at Verulanium (St Albans) to refute the Pelagian heresy. He himself had Celtic links coming from Brittany; St German's in Cornwall is named in his memory. Dewi was thus supporting the tradition defended by Germanus, a representative of the Western Church.

This combination of a strong defence of indigenous traditions with an appreciation of the orthodox teaching of the wider Church, points to the seeds of an early symbiosis of the local and the universal. It is a symbiosis that is expressed still more effectively in the seventh and eighth centuries by Gregory the Great, Theodore of Tarsus, and their successors. The creative tension manifested here clearly remained important even as late as the eleventh century when Rhygyvarch wrote his biography of Dewi. He too was concerned to defend the rights of the Welsh bishops and the integrity of the diocese of St Davids, this time over against the claims of St Anselm. Anselm, who became Archbishop of Canterbury in 1093, attempted – unsuccessfully – to bring all of Britain and Ireland under the provincial jurisdiction of Canterbury.

In the light of such claims, it is perhaps the local which we should celebrate in the memory of Dewi. Commentators reflect upon a set of values which were treasured and indeed may still be discovered in Welsh-speaking rural communities of west Wales. Such values include respect, earned by showing respect for others; lowliness in contrast to arrogance; a sense of being 'at home' with God and with one's neighbours; then finally a sense of 'belonging' which both defines the community and sets its own self-understanding and identity. Dewi's spirituality is richly captured in D. Gwenallt Jones's poem to the saint. This extract is a translation from the original, which is written in Welsh:

I saw Dewi strolling from county to county like God's gypsy, with the Gospel and the Altar in his caravan … to show us what is the purpose of learning. He went down to the bottom of the pit with the miners and cast the light of his wise lamp on the coal face; on the platform of the steel works he put on the goggles … and showed the Christian being purified like metal in the furnace … And after the Communion he talked to us about God's natural order, the person, the family, the nation and the society of nations, and the Cross keeping us from turning anyone one of them into a God.

Gwenallt's poem is a perfect transition for us from the antique world of Dewi's Romano-British Christians to the equally tough realities of our own society and culture. It is a potent reminder that in relating the local to the universal we must needs remember not only the ruggedness of the landscape, but also the realities of economics and the effects of a fast-changing culture. Both local and universal will always retain elements of stability alongside perpetual transformation; neither is ever present as an abstraction. Hence the well-known truism: 'Nothing is real unless it is local.' The universal is only possible if local communities exist. But the opposite is equally true. We cannot understand our own community if we do not also see ourselves as part of an interdependent common humanity. The person, the family, the nation and the society of nations – none of these must become a God. We all remain pilgrims both in time and in space.

HONOURING OUR LOCAL HERITAGE

Appreciating the local is effectively honouring the particular heritage into which we are born. Heritage all too easily gathers to itself something of the feeling of the idyll. It brings out echoes of stately homes, of national customs, of pageantry (often spurious) and of a static, immovable deposit of tradition. In Britain there is now even a senior Government Minister styled the 'Heritage Secretary'. The fact that that same person is responsible for the National Lottery (whatever our views on that may be) at least earths the concept of heritage. For our heritage is all that we owe to our predecessors and all that we hold in trust for each other. The cherishing of our heritage will thus include all the communities which flourish locally and it will include aspects of community that may seem to us to be novel and sometimes even alien to our own inheritance. Gwenallt's bringing together of the coal mines and steel works of South Wales with the memory of Dewi vividly focuses this for us.

Recent years have marked a new cherishing of local, regional and national traditions. Movements for devolution in Scotland and Wales have been prompted by a renewed realization of the culture and folk memories which stand behind Scottish and Welsh nationality. The Christian missions which underpin this cultural variety are part of what there is to celebrate. These missions helped form the culture, often by acting as a sharp critique to the values of a more jealous and power-seeking world. Wilfrid's exiles and Columba's pilgrimage for Christ off the shore of Brude's kingdom are both examples of this. Wilfrid's own loyalty to the wider Western Church was also a reminder that nationalism easily becomes a form of idolatry. The twentieth century is a historical canvas upon which numerous landscapes of such idolatry have been drawn. The tragic conflicts which ensued following the collapse of the Soviet Empire are a recent example.

But we do not need to go as far as Bosnia or Nagorno-Karabakh to discover such tragedies, nor indeed should we restrict our gaze to the twentieth century. The troubles in Northern Ireland, which began in 1969, bring together the perils of conflicting nationalisms with the danger of an uncritical allegiance to a particular religious tradition. Following the 1994 cease-fire in Northern Ireland, the Archbishop of Canterbury visited Armagh, Belfast, Derry, Dublin and Limerick. During an ecumenical service in Christ Church Cathedral, Dublin, the Archbishop asked the Irish people for forgiveness for the wrongs wrought over the centuries by the English. His plea brought mixed responses, although by far the majority of people applauded his words; indeed, it elicited from a number of Irish people an equal plea for forgiveness in the other direction. For some it helped rekindle a sense of common humanity. The engagement of the local with the universal is complex and it often provokes within us strong emotional reactions. A true symbiosis requires of us the ability to cherish our national and local inheritance at the same time as embracing the common humanity of which we are all part. The struggles to discern an appropriate model of European unity are another manifestation of the tension which lies at the heart of this symbiosis.

The cherishing of an inheritance locally is not confined to nationality nor even to a region, as in the case of Dyfed in the age of Dewi. The growth of cities and conurbations and the consequent depopulation of the countryside has led to further challenges to understandings of community within many industrialized nations. The growth of great cities with thriving commercial hearts was a symbol of prosperity as the industrial revolution transformed Western nations. In recent decades, however, the growth of cities has been overtaken by urban decay. Such decay has led to fragmentation within local communities and to new manifestations of poverty. One of the outflows of an enterprise culture is an unavoidable accent on individualism and a subsequent breakdown in community. At its most extreme this results in urban violence and even the depopulation of the inner city. The Christian gospel calls out of the churches a response to such conditions.

It was in the face of such challenges that David Sheppard, Derek Worlock and John Newton, church leaders in Liverpool, worked together for their city from the mid-1980s onward. It was also in the face of this crisis in local communities that the Archbishop of Canterbury commissioned a report on so-called 'urban priority areas'. The result was *Faith in the City*, which appeared in 1985. The commission was hard-hitting as some brief extracts from the report indicate:

Poverty is at the root of *powerlessness*. Poor people in Urban Priority Areas are at the mercy of fragmented and apparently unresponsive public authorities ... One way of seeking to understand these phenomena is as signs of an evident and apparently increasing *inequality* in our society ... Another possible analysis (which we shall make some use of ourselves) is in terms of *polarization* ... It is our considered view that the nation is confronted by a *grave and fundamental injustice* in the Urban Priority Areas.[1]

Reaction to the report by right-wing politicians was extremely hostile. It was dismissed as 'Marxist' and 'another example of the Church interfering with politics'. It was indicted for including no explicit theological analysis, even though the report itself was clearly dependent upon a number of implicit theological assumptions. But the commission argued: 'Doctrine is formulated, not in the abstract, but to settle questions already in dispute'; one of the overwhelming perceptions gained by members of the commission was of a society which is fragmented and indeed often polarized. Even where there are clear communities, they are often isolated from each other. The community living in North Lambeth and Vauxhall in the most 'inner-city' area of South London is a good working example.

In terms of housing, there is a mixture of Victorian villas and nineteenth-century artisan estates. Alongside these stand a number of inter-war blocks of flats and then more post-war flats, substantially higher, and replacing earlier bombed-out housing. The demography of the area is also varied. There is a large Afro-Caribbean community which is now the majority group. There is then a community of poor white people and also a substantial amount of gentrification within the Victorian estates and terraced villas. Industry is almost entirely dead in the area; some warehouses and derelict factories have been converted into studio flats. The population includes a number of professional people (MPs, lawyers and business people), and so 'effectively' there is a classical mixture of social groups. The crime rate is high, one parent families almost the norm in some parts of the area, and educational prospects are dismal.

Within this varied scenario a number of dedicated professionals work across social divisions, but the abiding feeling is of a series of disconnected communities living alongside each other. It is not that there is a denial of common humanity. Instead there is a sense of parallel existence and something of a fatalist inertia in the face of this fragmentation. Across the road from one area of derelict factories and under the shadow of post-war flats are situated an urban farm and a heritage centre, the latter set within the building of a splendid neo-Gothic Victorian church, which still supports a worshipping community on Sundays. The farm and the heritage centre focus the fragmentation instead of reducing it, since both institutions tend to draw middle-class people from within and well outside the area both to run them and as the 'customers'.

The area is still well served with churches: two Anglican, one Anglican-Methodist shared building, a United Reformed church, a Roman Catholic church and St George's Roman Catholic Cathedral. Although it would be wrong to claim too much for the churches, there is some truth in saying that they are one of the few places (except for the supermarkets, where social exchange is haphazard and casual) where some sense of wholeness can be experienced. Respect is shown for the integrity of the sub-groups: the black community and the white professionals each live fairly self-contained existences outside church worship. Even so, there is a real symbiosis within the congregations, however small, and of whatever church.

The situation described here is deliberately chosen, since it is worlds apart from that within which the early Christian missionaries to these islands spread the gospel. The urban centres within which Augustine, Mellitus and Paulinus ministered were but the living remains of Roman civilization. Fragmentation of these communities was still great. Tribalism mitigated against any moves toward a single kingdom or even a confederation. In the rural parts of northern England, or in Scotland and Ireland, small communities lived an even more isolated and fragmented existence. Within these places, local loyalties were fiercely defended; the story of Dewi's church in the face of Irish invasions makes the point well. Within such a world, the early missionaries sought to preach a gospel of wholeness and of life abundant. They brought a gospel, the initiation into which was through the sacrament of baptism, which made individuals part of the body of Christ. The sacrament that nourished them regularly throughout their lives was the eucharist. It was a corporate rite with 'all partaking of the one bread so that while being many they were one body' (1 Corinthians 10:17). The Gregorian mission and its inheritors were keen to stress the implications of this for the local church in relation to the universal. The greater Church and the local Church could not exist without each other. The implications for a fragmented contemporary world are obvious.

REDISCOVERING OUR COMMON HUMANITY

Alongside the tragic loss of life through two world wars and through numerous other conflicts and atrocities, the history of the twentieth century abounds in paradoxes. Both Hitler's National Socialism and Stalin's Marxist-Leninism succeeded in dividing the world more bitterly and more completely, perhaps, than at any other time in history. Churchill's coining of the image of the Iron Curtain, at his speech in Fulton, Missouri, after the Second World War captured the widespread feeling of a divided Europe. Yet, in paradoxical contrast to this, stands the emergence of the United Nations Organization and of the European Union which, despite their weaknesses, both testify to a greater sense of wholeness and interdependence within humanity than hitherto has been perceived. Often this rediscovery of our common humanity can be traced to the inspiration of the Christian gospel; Jean Monnet, for example, the architect of European unity, was a Roman Catholic inspired by the vision of the philosopher and theologian Jacques Maritain and others. Jacques Delors is a loyal Roman Catholic. Dietrich Bonhoeffer and George Bell, both tireless workers for peace and reconciliation, were first and foremost 'internationalists' working for the reconciliation of peoples even before they were co-workers for unity between the Churches.

The 'Ecumenical Movement', which traces its contemporary origins back to the Edinburgh Conference of 1910, also had some political and social origins. Three complementary movements were styled 'Life and Work', 'Faith and Order' and 'World Mission'. The foundation of the World Council of Churches in 1948 was a milestone ecumenically. Initially it drew together Life and Work and Faith and Order under one umbrella; the International Missionary Council was included later, at the New Delhi Assembly in 1961. At the heart of the ecumenical movement lies the desire to bring together the fragmented Christian Churches so that 'they might be perfectly one' (John 17:23), that the whole of God's Church might express the visible unity for which Christ prayed. The impulse toward unity issued from a dual theological commitment – to the one holy catholic and apostolic Church, and also to one common mission. That mission is expressed both in the direct proclamation of the gospel and through the implications of the gospel for peace, justice, reconciliation and wholeness in society. The problems addressed earlier in regard to the inner city are a direct outflow of this impulse for reconciliation and wholeness. There are clear resonances, albeit in utterly changed cultural circumstances, with the early Christian mission in these islands. Healing, wholeness, reconciliation and relief for the poor were at the heart of Cuthbert's mission in Northumbria. Wilfrid's theological commitment to the unity of the Church through one common tradition was paralleled by his primary concern for people's welfare. We saw this in his mission to the South Saxons. The universality to which Wilfrid was so firmly committed is the same vision as that of the contemporary ecumenical movement.

Some would argue that we have lost ground in allowing a separation between the two primary imperatives toward unity to persist. Almost fifty years on, there is still far too great a sense of theology and social ethics being carried on in two watertight compartments within the World Council of Churches (WCC). Justice, peace and the integrity of creation, which summarizes the social ethical strand within the WCC, is too rarely allowed to engage with the theological search for 'the unity which is both God's will and his gift'; the reverse is also true. The resultant dangers are obvious – social comment which is unrelated to an overtly theological foundation, or theology which is insufficiently rooted in the realities of a broken, violent and unjust world. Our acknowledgement of our common humanity and a realization of one universal Church are all part of one and the same imperative. This was the vision that fired Bonhoeffer and Bell, as it did Wilfrid and Gregory the Great.

Despite setbacks, significant steps have been taken towards a new appreciation of the universal which holds all of the local churches together in one common faith. The Decree of Ecumenism of the Second Vatican Council – *Unitatis Redintegratio* (1965) – was a milestone. It signalled that the largest Church in

Christendom, the Roman Catholic Church, was fully committed to the ecumenical process. Its acknowledgement that the Church 'subsists in' the Roman Catholic Church opened the door to recognizing true marks of the Church in other 'churches and ecclesial communities'. The subsequent meetings between the Pope and the Oecumenical Patriarch, which removed the centuries-old mutual anathemas, and between successive Popes and Archbishops of Canterbury and other Christian leaders, have deepened the Churches' commitment to each other. This process has been reinforced by the fruits of ecumenical theological dialogue. Such meetings and such dialogue have sought ways of expressing the universal nature of the Church without denying the significance and reality of the local church.[2]

The resonances between the aims of the contemporary search for unity with the aims of the synods during the early history of the churches in our islands is remarkable. The synods at Whitby and Hertford were not ultimately about the dating of Easter or the technicalities of episcopal jurisdictions but instead about the apostolic tradition. How could local patterns of observance remain in communion with the universal Church of Christ. Such questions stand at the heart of our continuing search for unity. One of the most remarkable agreements, that concluded in Lima in 1982 in the presence of more than one hundred theologians from across the Churches, on *Baptism, Eucharist and Ministry*,[3] has at its centre the question of the apostolic tradition:

The Church lives in continuity with the apostles and their proclamation ... The Spirit keeps the Church in the apostolic tradition until the fulfilment of history in the Kingdom of God. Apostolic tradition in the Church means continuity in the permanent characteristics of the Church of the apostles.

Obviously at the heart of this lies the apostolic faith and also both the sacraments and ministry whereby that faith is passed on to new generations. The ministry has also been that means whereby communion has been sustained and local churches have related to each other. The concern of Gregory, Theodore, Wilfrid and Boniface over relations with the Holy See directly relate to this. We see in Boniface a good example of an emphasis on the province (the local) combined with a recognition of the universal. Recent ecumenical dialogue has attempted to rediscover an appropriate recognition of universality: the Lima document talks of the bishop in the classical manner as the 'focus of unity' in the local church; following the Second Vatican Council, the Roman Catholic Church has recognized collegiality among the bishops – the Church is a community of communities; the Anglican-Roman Catholic dialogue has moved one further step down this road in recognizing the need for some form of primacy which focuses on the universal nature of the Church. The primacy envisaged here reflects the same intentions which we discovered in seventh-century Europe. The statement on authority notes:

> ... communion with the bishop of Rome does not imply submission to an authority which would stifle the distinctive features of the local churches ... primacy, rightly understood, implies that the bishop of Rome exercises his oversight in order to guard and promote the faithfulness of all the Churches to Christ and one another.[4]

Although Anglicans, Roman Catholics and other Christian churches do not yet share sufficiently their understanding of the nature of the Church to allow for the exercise of such a primacy amongst all Christians, nevertheless the aspiration presents a noble goal. The desire to retain local distinctiveness within a world-wide communion, appropriate provincial freedom with a universal pattern of authority, liturgical variety within the bounds of an agreed set of rites is a direct response to the historic traditions into which we have been born. Where wisdom and forbearance ruled, this was the precise result as the two missionary roots grew together – the example of Theodore is evidence enough.

INCORRIGIBLE PLURALITY

Despite all that we have described, there is a tendency within Western culture at present to abhor authority and limiting structures. Louis MacNeice wrote:

> World is crazier and more of it than we think,
> Incorrigibly plural. I peel and portion
> A tangerine and spit the pips and feel
> The drunkenness of things being various.

The plurality which MacNeice describes is undeniable. It applies as much to Christianity as it does to other aspects of culture. But plurality is no new phenomenon, even if we now see it in rather more exaggerated forms. The New Testament bears witness to a considerable plurality. Indeed some of the Letters of Paul touch upon how far such pluralism might be allowed to go. Paul addresses the rivalry between different groups – some are for Paul, some for Apollos and some follow Cephas (Peter) – responding to such factions using the image of God's building where each of us is a crucial part. He talks of us also as fellow workers in God's garden (1 Corinthians 3:9). The symbiosis between the part and the whole is still there.

Even those subjects about which the New Testament appears to speak with a consistent voice have an inner complexity. One example here is the central concept of love. The word used (in Greek *agape*) describes love in a unique way for Christian people; it is not self-regarding love, but instead is rooted in self-giving. Even so, the exercise of that love within the earliest Christian communities varied. In Luke's Gospel it is quite clear that such love is all embracing and reaches out beyond the confines of the Christian community to include all who previously were felt to be outcast. Such was the case with the good Samaritan (Luke 10:25–37), the prodigal son (Luke 15:11–32) and the tax-collector (Luke 18:9–14). Those belonging to the Johannine community, however, were far more exclusive in their exercise of love; it is that which binds together the community. The First Letter of John makes this clear throughout and particularly in the fourth chapter; it is their fellow Christians whom the brethren are to love (1 John 3:14,23; 4:7,11,20–21).

This brief glance at the New Testament makes it clear that plurality was part of the Christian community's experience from earliest times. James Dunn, in a study of unity and diversity in the New Testament, comes to the conclusion that although there is a unifying strand which holds together the proclamation of the gospel in the New Testament communities, nevertheless: 'In different situations the actual gospel was different and could be as different as the situations themselves ... it would not have been possible to abandon [these differences] in the situation which called forth that particular form of proclamation without altering its character as good news to that situation'.[5] It was this same phenomenon that the missionaries of the eighth century encountered in each others' communities; the gospel had adapted itself to that situation and sometimes in very practical ways, as in the different approaches to mission and in the different ways of exercising episcopacy.

The implication of this continuing experience is not then that plurality is itself either new or threatening. MacNeice is right in describing 'the drunkenness of things being various' and the 'incorrigible plurality' of the world. The issue is of how the Christian Church should respond to such plurality. How can we do justice to the contingency and relativity of each time and place without letting go of what Dunn describes as the distinctive character of the gospel. Certainly Western churches have been guilty of exporting the gospel to all parts of the world in a form which bears the clearest imprint of our own cultural assumptions and with little or no adaptation. Almost twenty years ago now, Vincent Donovan, a Roman Catholic priest and missionary, rebelled against this approach and argued for a far more open approach. It was to be simply a matter of telling the gospel story and then leaving it to bear fruit in the community:

> Having explained not only what Jesus said, but, even more important, what he is and had done to him, I finished the story of Christ for the Masai ... This was the end of the good news I had come to proclaim to the Masai. The response to it was up to them.

Later he expands the point relating it to the lifestyle of the Masai:

> I looked at these Masai sons and daughters of the plains and wondered what possible image they would have of the church that had come among them. These nomads had no church buildings, no shrines, no tabernacles ... For them it would always have to be a pilgrim church.[6]

TRANSFORMATION AND TRADITION

Donovan deliberately poses the question in its most extreme form. Taken at its word, such a process could sow the seeds for numerous communities throughout the world whose roots lay in the Christian gospel, but whose identities might offer very few resonances with the tradition as we have received it, and as it is lived by mainstream Christian churches throughout the world. Yet his central thesis cannot be ignored. For wherever the gospel is planted, the texture and make-up of the soil, the climate, and the landscape will all affect its growth. There will be a distinctiveness about different Christian traditions that will change and develop depending upon the culture and the location.

Donovan continued to reflect upon the significance of the ministry and his reflections appear to be determined partly by the response of the Masai and by his own understanding of priesthood. The Masai themselves seemed to believe that the priest is the one who can bring the community into existence and without whom the Christian community can neither exist nor function. Not all Christian traditions would state it thus, but this does focus the significance of continuity and communion, of a distinctiveness that is not cut totally free from the universal.

This returns us both to the roots of Christian mission in our islands and also to our own day. Columba, Patrick, Augustine and Dewi each found themselves ministering in a particular place, and each was the product of a living tradition. That tradition had been variously shaped and transformed but it still focused upon Christ, whose ministry these missionaries shared. Dewi's monastery at St Davids lives on in the cathedral that bears his name, but the wider setting is now transformed. Within twenty miles of that sacred place are the oil refineries of Milford Haven, the ferry port in Fishguard and the tank ranges of the Pembrokeshire coast near Castlemartin. The changed landscape and society will demand new clothes for the gospel, a changed apologetic, but it is not a different gospel nor a different Lord.

The Christian Church walks a narrow tightrope. Donovan's reflections capture the dilemma movingly and dramatically. Retreat too far from the black communities of North Lambeth, in the interests of their own freedom, and you have ceased to exercise a real un-self-regarding love; the fragmentation which is a trademark of late twentieth century Western culture is then imprinted even upon Christian congregations. But insist upon the cultural norms of Elizabethan society as set out in the Book of Common Prayer, and resentment or sheer incomprehension will shut the black communities out. It is a salutary warning and it applies to all our communities, black and white, affluent and poor.

The struggles between authentic indigenous traditions and a universal gospel in the early centuries were never lost or won. The same tension lives on as the Vatican negotiates with local churches throughout the world, as united free churches establish themselves in various parts of the world, and as Anglicans attempt to find appropriate models for communion and authority across the world. Symbiosis between local and universal will never be easy and never without tension. Living with patience, however, the Church may offer a mission as effective and varied as that which transformed life in these islands. That is at the heart of the experience of a pilgrim Church.

Prayer

Almighty Creator, who has made all things,
The world cannot express all your glories,
Even though the grass and the trees should sing.

The Father has wrought so great a multitude of wonders
That they cannot be equalled.
No letters can contain them, no letters can express them.

He who made the wonder of the world
Will save us, has saved us.
It is not too great toil to praise the Trinity.

Purely, humbly, in skilful verse
I should delight to give praise to the Trinity.
It is not too great toil to praise the Son of Mary.

> *Amen.*

Ninth-century Welsh prayer – from the Juvencus
manuscript, Cambridge.

SEVEN

MISSIONARY PILGRIMS

The Irish and Roman patterns offered variety in mission which itself demonstrated a richness in their different understandings of the underlying theology of God's providence.

CORNISH CHRISTIANITY

I knelt in darkness at St Enodoc;
I visited our local Holy Well,
Whereto the native Cornish still resort
For cures for whooping cough, and drop bent pins
Into its peaty water ...
... Not a sign:
No mystical experience was vouchsafed ...
But somewhere, somewhere underneath the dunes,
Somewhere among the cairns or in the caves
The Celtic saints would come to me, the ledge
Of time we walk on, like a thin cliff-path
High in the mist, would show the precipice.

John Betjeman's love of Cornwall went back to his childhood, to his encounters with the local priest who would talk of poetry and Cornish saints. Perhaps more than anywhere else in

Britain or Ireland, Cornwall evokes for the visitor the enigmas and mysteries of an irrecoverable Christian past. Apart from some wayside crosses, there are few buildings or artefacts to tell the story of those far-off days. One exception to this is St Piran's oratory. The modern pilgrim must journey across the sand dunes from Perranporth to the inauspicious concrete tunnel which was built early this century to protect the chapel. The journey is rewarding, for here in this desolate place are the remains of the oratory of a Celtic monastery. It was built towards the end of the fifth century to house Piran's relics and to act as his shrine. Piran was patron of Cornish tinners and his cult flourished both in Wales and in Brittany; he was a pilgrim missionary to the Dumnonii, the tribal group living in Cornwall before the Roman invasion, coming from either Ireland or Wales.

The prefix 'Lan', which is found in many Cornish place names, refers to a monastic enclosure; enclosed would have been a series of huts grouped around an oratory; St Piran's oratory most likely stood at the centre of just such a monastery. The huts were the monks' cells, who in the early days of Celtic monasticism would have come to study at the feet of a great teacher. Eventually, greater monasteries developed and the leader became the abbot and, as we have seen, also sometimes a bishop. Such monasteries were centres of missionary activity, and the later significance of both Bodmin and St Germans suggests that they were the sites of great monasteries and through this became Christian centres.

Development of Christian mission in Cornwall, then, took a distinctive form, albeit within the wider Celtic tradition; some 170 local saints date from this early missionary period. This in itself gave Cornish Christianity a distinctive flavour. The persistence of this distinctiveness was assured by the fact that in far-off Cornwall, the edicts of the Synod of Whitby had no effect. The Church continued on its own path, observing Easter according to the Celtic pattern. It was not until after the appeal from Aldhelm in 705, when the pressure from the Saxons was becoming irresistible, that things began to change, although formal submission to the authority of Canterbury did not come until 850.

We should not, however, see even this as the end of the distinctiveness of Cornish Christianity. As we have seen elsewhere, the embracing of the jurisdiction of Canterbury and through Canterbury of the papal universal jurisdiction of the Western Church did not lead to uniformity. Indeed, local customs and rites would eventually enrich the wider Church. The extraordinary catalogue of local saints survived not only in the dedication of churches, but also in the towns and villages which grew up around them.

In the eighteenth century, with the advent of the Industrial Revolution, Methodism made its impact in Cornwall. At its height, Methodism was *de facto* the established religion of the Cornish people. Wesley himself preached in Cornwall. Perhaps the most remarkable Cornish shrine to him is Gwennap Pit. In this extraordinary amphitheatre, cut into the side of Carn Math between Gwennap and Redruth, Wesley preached to twenty thousand people. Wesley's unusual blend of a profound and stirring spiritual experience together with the ability to tap an uninhibited folk religion, touched the hearts of the poor. Particularly with the new industrial poor, he was able to arouse and direct the implicit religion which he discovered to be part of every human soul. Wesley broke through the formality of the established religion of the time and unashamedly became a field preacher. It was George Whitefield who had finally convinced him of this necessity. He wrote in his *Journal* for 31 March 1739, on meeting Whitefield near Bristol:

I could scarce reconcile myself at first to this strange way of preaching in the fields, of which he set me an example on Sunday; having been all my life (till very lately) so tenacious of every point relating to decency and order, that I should have thought the saving of souls almost a sin, if it had not been done in church.

Two days later he puts it still more graphically:

At four in the afternoon, I submitted to be more vile, and proclaimed in the highways the glad tidings of salvation, speaking from a little eminence in a ground adjoining the city, to about three thousand people.

A new pattern of mission was thus established, and the Methodism which grew most vigorously in Cornwall, that of the Bible Christians, was again distinctive. The Bible Christians were founded by one William O'Bryan, a Cornishman of Irish descent who was himself a fervent preacher. Such was his zeal and so itinerant was he that he failed to submit to the fairly authoritarian Methodist connectional regulations and he was expelled. In fact, the first Bible Christians were not really Methodists in the strict sense; their religion appealed more to the emotions than Wesleyan Methodism. Its most famous (and even infamous) distinctive marks were that it gave full authorisation to women itinerant preachers and it encouraged the evangelistic exploits of Billy Bray, previously a notorious drunkard and lecher. Bray, a converted tin miner, remains one of the heroes of early Cornish Methodism. In an utterly different way, contemporary to the revivalism of the times, the Bible Christians mirrored the courage, evangelistic fervour, and pilgrim spirit of the early Celtic missionaries to the ancient kingdom of Lyonnesse, the land of the Dumnonii.

BOUNDARIES TO MISSION?

Cornwall, both in ancient and recent times, is illustrative of the varieties of mission patterns that we have already encountered in our journey of discovery through the seventh century. There are distinguishing characteristics which mark off the Cornish experience from Christianity elsewhere. This should not surprise us. The missions of Patrick, Ninian, Dewi, Columba, Wilfrid and Aidan all have their trademarks. The landscape itself is to some degree determinative, as is the culture of the people, yet there are, however, common strands.

One of these is the reliance of the Celtic Church on a monastic pattern, when the Gregorian missionaries (and particularly after Theodore) relied upon a more strictly territorial pattern. Put crudely, the Roman bishops were keen to mark out areas of responsibility and jurisdiction. The principle of boundaries looms large. Even now this inheritance persists. Within Anglicanism, for example, there are occasionally disputes between clergy and parishes who operate a strict baptism policy and those who would be seen almost as pirates and predators. Within the parish where a strict baptism policy operates there are clear and exacting demands made upon parents asking for baptism for infants. Commitment must be clear; churchgoing for a specified and sometimes long period is a requirement. Nearby parishes may be just as extreme in requiring no clear commitment whatsoever from those asking for baptism. Moreover, they may be prepared to baptize the children of dissidents from nearby parishes where the regime is strict. The potential for conflict is manifest, and the significance of boundaries paramount.

It is argued that these local disputes in the contemporary Church can be traced back to a fundamental divergence in the mission patterns exercised by the Celtic and Roman missionaries to Britain in the seventh century. Stated starkly it runs like this: the Gregorian missionaries worked from the first with the social structures they encountered, co-operating with the king's court and conquering by stealth. The bishop, under this model, became the adviser to the king or tribal chieftain. With Theodore's reforms, this pattern was extended to produce a comprehensive network of parishes based upon the towns, villages and hamlets in a particular geographical region, where the parish priests were under the jurisdiction of the local bishop. The structure for this is clearly recorded by Bede in his account of the Synod of Hertford. These structures were underpinned by canon law, as Bede's account makes clear.

The Celtic approach is painted as being very different to this. Here, monastic communities were the spiritual power-houses from which monks would make aggressive forays into a heathen and unfriendly countryside. The bishop was himself a missionary and part of the monastic community. Sometimes, as we have seen, he would be the abbot, and on other occasions he would be a monk under obedience to the abbot. The monastery or minster would, on this model, be the centre for mission for the surrounding area. Bede again records canons of the Synod of Hertford which seek to set boundaries:

> ... monks shall not wander from place to place, that is from monastery to monastery, except with letters dismissory from their own abbot ... no clergy shall leave their own bishop and wander about at will, nor be received anywhere without letters of commendation from their own bishop.

How accurately, then, does this reflect the truth of the two situations, or indeed the necessities behind the mission of the Church either then or now? First of all we need to remind ourselves of the presuppositions which stand behind Bede's account. Bede is unashamedly part of the Roman observance and is keen to press his readers to accept the importance of a universal Western Church focused upon the Papacy. In doing so, the two patterns, the Irish and the Gregorian, are easily caricatured. Even a gentle pealing away of Bede's varnish suggests a more complex and overlapping reality. Bede admires the Irish missionaries; they are never pilloried or dismissed. Indeed, the Irish accepted the primacy of Rome. It was simply that the Irish pattern, as we have already seen, remained more firmly rooted in the monasteries, since this pattern was better adapted to the rural world in which the missionaries aimed to spread and nurture the gospel.

The notion of monastery should not, however, be read simply in terms of the later Benedictine models which have so influenced (and indeed enriched) the Western Church. Benedictine communities, and those which draw their model originally from the Benedictine Rule, are tight-knit. The principle of *stabilitas* holds the monks within the monastery and gives it a clear definition in relation to wider society. The Celtic model was very different from this. The pattern which was described in the communities which grew up around St Piran and St Petroc in Cornwall would not have been atypical of the Celtic model. The holy man would teach and live a life of prayer. Disciples would gather round him and the entire locality would be caught up into a monastic space within which the ministry and mission of the holy man and his disciples would predominate. Although the pattern is not immediately parochial, the contrast is by no means total. There is still a sense of the church ministering within a locality, even if it was not always as sharply defined as a parish. Indeed, even parishes within the Roman pattern would not have been as clearly bounded as the diocesan maps would now legislate for the contemporary Church.

If the geographical contrast is less sharp than might first appear, then so was the pattern of episcopal oversight. Bishops did have more territorial definition to their ministry than is often assumed. The episcopal inheritance in Wales is now accepted as having survived following the collapse of the Roman Empire. Even in Ireland there were dioceses, monasteries and embryonic parish patterns all standing alongside each other. Almost certainly the degree of territorial diocesan organization would have depended upon both political and demographic factors. Political changes led to changes in demography. The urban patterns established by the Romans collapsed as the Empire decayed and the organization of the Church subsequently adapted. The final result was far less tidy than the popular contrast between Celtic and Roman patterns now often suggests. Clearly there were differences in approach, but it is less easy to argue that one was either superior to or in competition with the other. Indeed, they often appear to be complementary.

Allowing for the distinctive flavour which the monastic tradition gave to the Celtic tradition, it is not at all clear that the missionary methods were as they are so often portrayed, that is forays out into unfriendly territory with an aggressively proclaimed gospel. We have seen that there certainly is such a strand within the Celtic tradition. Martin of Tours, Columbanus and others were often swift to obliterate earlier pagan temples and customs; such methods which involved eradicating the old ways could even mean resorting to violence. None the less, uncompromising methods were not restricted to the missionaries from Gaul or from Ireland. It seems likely that even Gregory the Great himself had rethought his position from one which was more confrontational to the pagan past to that which proposed a policy of Christianization of pagan sites.

We have alluded to similar episodes at Kildare amongst Irish missionaries. The stories of St Brigid are a tangled weave of pagan magic and Christian miracle. The strong sense of affirmation of the motherland which one encounters in the Celtic writers would suggest that a more nuanced approach to their pre-Christian forebears would have been reasonably common amongst the Celtic missionaries. Celtic Christianity was profoundly affected by and dependent upon the prevalent culture and thus often displays many continuities with the earlier tribal religions. The missionaries were prepared to appreciate the wish of a community to give thanks for the gifts of the earth, and indeed all natural gifts. The aim would be to woo people away from these earlier customs and endow the particular sacred site with a rededication to Jesus Christ.

The picture which has emerged from these reflections is more subtle than is often suggested. Both patterns of mission in the seventh century did have concerns with boundaries, inasmuch as a particular bishop or a particular monastery (or indeed both) would feel a responsibility for the evangelization of a certain piece of territory. It is unlikely that in cases where either the diocesan or the monastic pattern predominated the boundaries would be either clearly marked or seen as unchanging. Similar caveats need to be made about the suggestion that the boundaries of the pagan world were sharper for one tradition than for the other. Undoubtedly there were differences in emphasis, but these differences were not invariable within either of the two traditions, nor were they impatient of change.

IS GOD BEFORE OR AMONGST US?

Underlying so many of the discussions of mission which one encounters are different, and sometimes opposed, understandings of the nature of God's activity and his providence. In those cases where it is believed that the Christian evangelist is a soldier sent out into hostile territory to proclaim the gospel, the assumption appeared to be that God is locked in mortal combat with a personal devil, or that he is utterly absent from the landscape before the arrival of the missionaries. There is a hierarchy of evil spirits under the command of Satan against whom the Christian is bidden to do battle. Such a landscape becomes increasingly less credible as fewer and fewer people believe in any form of personified devil.

Although this landscape of a continuing mortal battle between supernatural beings of good and evil has now receded from our gaze, the aggressive presentation of the Christian story has not. Evil, seen in classical terms as the privation of good, clearly exists, and so still there is the need to make God present where previously God was absent.

But there is a different approach too, already hinted at in the early missions to their lands. It would be wrong to read into the seventh century Christian Church views that were not then yet explored, but it does seem that some missionary methods assumed that God was already working within the fabric of people's daily experience even before the gospel was preached. Hence we see pagan shrines associated with healing powers of the earlier gods being taken over as Christian sites. The implication is that God is capable of being made known through such places through the process of transformation from pagan to Christian observance. This reminds us of St Paul's words on the Areopagus:

Men of Athens, I see that in everything that concerns religion you are uncommonly scrupulous. As I was going round looking at the objects of your worship, I noticed among other things an altar bearing the inscription 'To an Unknown God'. What you worship but do not know – this is what I now proclaim. (Acts 17:22–23)[1]

This introduction to the gospel via an implicit religion then is hardly new, but it will always assume a particular importance where the dominant ethos is not explicitly religious or Christian. For this reason it has become particularly important in an increasingly secularized world. Both Celtic and Roman missionaries at different points saw this, in their attitude to evangelization.

Central to the proclamation of the Christian gospel, too, are attributes to the doctrines of *creation* and *redemption*. Creation refers not only to God's act in giving birth to the universe 'out of nothing'. It refers, too, to the continued sustaining of the universe, what the General Thanksgiving from the Book of Common Prayer refers to as 'our creation, preservation, and all the blessings of this life'. The doctrine of creation commits each believer to faith in the continuing activity of God in the world. In that sense, Christian mission is not a matter of bringing God to a godless world, but rather seeking to discover God's involvement and present activity in the world.

The doctrine of redemption is also essential. Understandably it receives greater emphasis where crisis or conflict threaten or where there is oppression or injustice, in other words, where redemption is a vital need. It is no accident, for example, that there was something of a re-emphasis upon human sin and the need for redemption at the end of the appalling suffering following the Great War.[2] Similarly, the growth of liberation theology in the late 1960s, in countries where unjust and oppressive regimes were in power, particularly in South and Central America and South Africa, also reflects such trends. The General Thanksgiving refers to the doctrine of redemption in equally fulsome terms, when it talks of the gifts of God and '... above all, for thine inestimable love in the redemption of the world by Our Lord Jesus Christ'. Human communities and individuals cry out for liberation or salvation from the various forms of alienation which press upon them.

We can learn similar lessons for our own understanding of the apologetic task in our contemporary world from those who spread the gospel in the seventh century. The Celtic tradition was particularly sensitive to the world of nature and thus to the doctrine of creation. We have already encountered Caedmon's writings at Whitby. The *Carmina Gadelica*, although collected in the last century, reflects a similar tradition which stretches back to the time of Columba, Aidan and Cuthbert. The awareness of the landscape within which they were placed and attachment to their particular country reinforced this love for creation. But it would be wrong to trace all of this emphasis on creation back to landscape alone. Worship also contributed, for a further source for reflection was the daily recitation of the psalms and canticles. Many psalms give thanks for the natural world and God's sustaining of it. In Psalm 24, we read: 'The earth is the Lord's, and all that therein is; the compass of the world and they that dwell therein.' Similar themes are reflected again and again. The psalms and canticles formed a balanced diet from the Celtic and Roman traditions alike. In the daily office, both creation and salvation canticles remain central. Morning Prayer included the *Venite*: 'In his hand are all the corners of the earth; and the strength of the hills is his also. The sea is his, and he made it: and his hands prepared the dry land' (Psalm 95:4–5). The *Te Deum* is a great hymn of praise for creation and redemption, the *Benedicite Omnia Opera* another hymn to creation and the *Benedictus* a hymn of thanksgiving for salvation. The canticles for Evening Prayer show a similar balance.

The richness, then, of both the Celtic and Roman traditions offers much not only through the methods practised by those who brought the gospel, but also by the underlying theology implied. The Celtic tradition certainly included a refreshing realization of God's blessing through his creation. But there was no ignoring of the gospel of salvation. If Martin of Tours, Columbanus and others used strong and even violent imagery, and indeed sought to eradicate the old heathen ways, it was because they believed humanity to be in mortal peril. The gospel of salvation must be preached if that same humanity was to have the opportunity of entering God's promised kingdom, the gates of which had been opened to all through the redemption made available in Jesus Christ. Over-romanticized pictures of the Celtic emphasis on creation do an injustice to the balanced nature of the gospel proclaimed by Cuthbert and his followers. They also lay the tradition open to being used in a manner which too easily embraces the eclecticism of certain modern religious movements. They drive an inappropriate wedge between the Celtic and Roman ways.

The Celtic way did offer a distinctive colour to the gospel which embraced creation and celebrated the landscape in which it flourished. In doing so it contributed to the various patterns of mission that attracted the searching pilgrims to the Christian gospel.

KALEIDOSCOPIC MISSION

In talking of pilgrims searching for the Christian gospel, one is immediately begging a number of questions. When does a seeker become a pilgrim? Is it that we are seeking God or that God is seeking us? Perhaps this final question is the most important of all. Clearly there within Judaeo-Christian tradition are both emphases. God seeks us out. God reveals himself to us in the person of Jesus Christ; this revelation is then attested to and responded to in the New Testament and also in the continuing tradition of the Church. But, as a tradition, it reaches down deep into the fertile traditions of ancient Israel. The

Psalmist often records such instincts. Psalm 139 states it classically in the Coverdale translation: 'O Lord, thou has searched me out and known me: thou knowest my down-sitting, and mine up-rising: thou understandest my thoughts long before.' It is there, too, in the famous encounter between Samuel and the Lord God, as Samuel sleeps in the Temple (1 Samuel 3). The Lord seeks Samuel out and declares his prophetic vocation.

But alongside this tradition there is an equally noble pattern of pilgrims seeking the Lord. Again it is there clearly in the Psalter. In Psalm 71, the writer reflects: 'For thou, O Lord God art the thing that I long for: thou art my hope, even from my youth.' The same experience is expressed classically in the words of St Augustine of Hippo, when eventually he encounters Christ: 'Late, late have I loved thee, O beauty so old and yet so new, but now I have found thee, here in my heart.' This oscillation between the experience of the seeker and the God who seeks stands at the heart of all theological reflection. Often a distinction has been drawn between natural and revealed theology. *Revealed* theology relates to the corpus of revelation classically canonized in the Old and New Testaments. *Natural* theology refers to humanity's capacity to reflect upon both the natural order and human experience, and in both to be confronted by the existence of God. Sometimes these two approaches are placed in contrast to each other, even to the extent of denying the possibility of one or the other.[3] Experience, both from Scripture and tradition and from contemporary evidence, denies the need for such mutual exclusion. Instead it is a reciprocal movement of God and humanity toward each other. It is crystallized in the language of reflexivity employed by St Paul in his letter to the Romans:

In the same way the Spirit comes to the aid of our weakness. We do not even know how we ought to pray, but through our inarticulate groans the Spirit himself is pleading for us, and God who searches our inmost being knows what the Spirit means, because he pleads for God's people as God himself wills; and in everything, as we know, he co-operates for good with those who love God and are called according to his purpose. (Romans 8:26–28)

This very same reflexivity is clear from both the methods and from the writings of the earliest missionaries to these islands. Traditions of pilgrimage during this period confirm this reflexivity. St Columbanus, perhaps the most persistent voyager and pilgrim, talked of the Christian soul as a 'guest of the world'. Pilgrimage is that which we encountered in our first chapter, a sense of journeying to one's true home. It is a matter, says Columbanus, of seeking the place of one's resurrection. Pilgrimage applies to both those who have just begun the journey (or indeed have only just realized that such a journey might be possible), and to those who have discovered or been discovered by God, and now seek their true home. This was the resonance most often captured in the Irish tradition, as Nora Chadwick summarizes it: '... those who have made pilgrimage and exile in the world, just as the elders who went before'.[4]

The subtlety and complexity of the picture which is suggested by different patterns and models of pilgrimage, and by the reflexivity in our relationship to God argues for a kaleidoscopic approach to the mission of the Church. It commends to us sufficient variety such that we may work with God in the world where God is already present, but also be prepared to confront people with the message of the gospel when necessary. Both of these approaches require of us discernment and then energy, and both of them may lead us into conflict with the mores of the time.

In the first case, *Faith in the City*, to which we referred earlier, implied that God is already present even in the most deprived parts of our inner cities. We are given the responsibility to work with him both as individuals and within institutions. The American theologian Reinhold Niebuhr talked of 'common grace', the presence and power of God made available through society and through institutions. In the second case, we might look to individuals like Dietrich Bonhoeffer and George Bell, or groups like those who produced the 'Kairos Document' in 1985 in South Africa. Bonhoeffer's unstinting efforts to make the German churches aware of the evils of the Nazi regime, and Bell's work with him (together with his condemnation of obliteration bombing) brought them both into conflict with their own establishments and indeed even into conflict with conventional moral positions on tyrannicide and just war. The framers of the 'Kairos Document' similarly took up a prophetic stance on behalf of the churches in relation to the evils of apartheid.

Already, then, we have begun to uncover some of the variety which should result from a kaleidoscopic view of mission. What different approaches might be seen through the eyepiece of the kaleidoscope? They include the parochial and monastic models which trace their origins to the early missions. There is the model of 'field preaching' which we encountered in Wesley, in the Bible Christians and which has been a familiar feature of revivalist movements ever since. There is also the tradition of prophecy and engagement with social issues, which is itself an integral part of the Church's ministry (in other words social responsibility and justice and peace are not a luxury to be axed when ecclesiastical finances are running low); that other aspect of mission which includes events (some repeated annually), street theatre and pilgrimages. This list is by no means comprehensive, but it gives some feel for the variety of approaches to mission which are best seen as complementary rather than as alternatives, as different approaches for different times and people, and not mutually exclusive models.

As enthusiasm for a renewed Celtic mission has gained ground, so has the parish model been seen by some as too monolithic and inflexible. And yet the vision pioneered by Theodore is noble and indeed universal in scope.

> Soon after his arrival, [Theodore] visited every part of the island occupied by the English peoples, and received a ready welcome and hearing everywhere ... The people eagerly sought the new-found joys of the kingdom of heaven, and all who wished for instruction in the reading of the Scriptures found teachers ready at hand.

Bede's account both here and elsewhere is unashamedly admiring of Theodore's work, and it communicates clearly the intentions and strengths of the parochial system's geographical and human universality. None falls outside the care of the Christian community. The occasional offices relating to the rites of passage at birth, marriage and death are the most central focus of this. This universality will imply an inclusivity to the Church's mission where those responsible as ministers welcome people by offering to them the rites of the Church demonstrating that the whole world is God's. The fragmentary nature of contemporary life is offered a context for meaning in God. Wesley Carr argues for this with great cogency. He notes: 'The minister is viewed as God's representative (the servant), one who enables people, through the way in which he treats them and allows them to treat him, hold together their fragmented experience of their present existence.'[5]

The monastic (or minster) tradition has again been lauded as we have rediscovered Celtic roots. It is both a flexible and multi-faceted approach to mission and offers us the model of centres of excellence, specialism and vision standing alongside the mode of geographical universality. Religious orders, with whom this tradition began, are perhaps now undervalued or easily forgotten. Within the Roman Catholic tradition they remain an essential part of the Church's mission. But Anglicanism and the Protestant tradition have also recovered the religious life. Both the contemplative/eremitic and the itinerant or mendicant traditions still offer to the world a countercultural model which challenges the received values of wider society. Cathedrals, too, are an invaluable resource. They remain one of the places where people of any religion or none come as tourists but also often as seekers; the candles lit in these ancient buildings testify to people's continuing search for meaning and to their belief in the loving purpose of God.

Finally, the influence of pilgrimage, events and street theatre ought not to pass us by. In recent years, the Taizé Community in France and festivals like 'Greenbelt' and 'Spring Harvest' have annually brought together young people, offering them a sense of community of faith often lacking in a fragmented world. Both the anonymity of great cities and the depopulation of the countryside have undermined community, and the young particularly often feel an acute sense of isolation which can attract them to less wholesome ways of receiving stimulation and identifying a sense of belonging. Pilgrimage can offer similar patterns of community and the regular journeys to Walsingham, Lourdes or again Taizé reflect this. Street theatre in Holy Week – processions or presentations of 'The Way of the Cross' – offer yet another means of bringing before people the gospel story and allowing it to relate to their own experience.

The distinctiveness and yet also the variety which we encountered in the Cornish saints, in Cornish Methodism and also in the patterns preserved there in the mainstream churches is a good introduction to the variety of patterns in Christian mission, patterns which existed even in earliest times. In that sense there are no boundaries to mission. Where there are boundaries, around parishes, dioceses, monastic communities or cathedral closes, they are only appropriately there if they aim to equip all God's people to proclaim a gospel to the whole world, where no individual or community feels excluded or forgotten by their Creator and Redeemer through the mission of the Church.

Prayer

We are no longer our own, but yours.
Put us to what you will, rank us with whom you will;
put us to doing, put us to suffering;
let us be employed for you or laid aside for you,
exalted for you or brought low for you;
let us be full, let us be empty;
let us have all things, let us have nothing;
We freely and wholeheartedly yield all things to your
*   pleasure and disposal.*
And now, glorious and blessed God,
Father, Son, and Holy Spirit,
you are ours and we are yours.
So be it.
And the covenant which we have made on earth,
let it be ratified in heaven. Amen.

From the Methodist Covenant Service

EIGHT

A GOSPEL OF WHOLENESS

Both early missionary traditions offered visions of unity and integrity. Such a vision transformed by the circumstances of our times stands at the centre of Christian life.

KENTIGERN'S BELOVED GREEN PLACE

I belong to Glasgow,
Dear old Glasgow town,
Oh, there's something the matter with Glasgow
For it's going round and round.
Now I'm only a common old working lad
As anyone here can see,
But when I've had a couple of pints on a Saturday,
Glasgow belongs to me.

The rollicking strains of the old music-hall song hardly conjure up in one's mind 'Kentigern's beloved green place' which is said to have been the origin of the Celtic word Glagu, Glasgu, or Gleschow, the root of the modern name Glasgow (other sources suggest that it may have referred to Kentigern's monastic foundation and that it meant 'Dear Community' or even 'Happy Family'). The music-hall song does, however, capture

146

the stereotype that many people in the past have had of Glasgow. It was pictured as a hard-working, hard-drinking city built upon the foundations of shipbuilding and other heavy industries. It was tough and almost synonymous with the word tenement, at least until the post-Second World War period, when areas of notorious slums, classically symbolized by the Gorbals, were replaced with some equally disastrous housing developments.

The image of Glasgow, however, has now changed radically. The virtual collapse of the shipbuilding industry and the need to develop new sources of prosperity has transformed Glasgow into a thriving commercial centre with one of the busiest international airports in Britain outside London. The locating of the remarkable Burrell art collection in its own purpose-designed building in the southern part of the city; the realization of the genius of one of Glasgow's most famous protégés, architect Charles Rennie Mackintosh, exemplified by his stunningly innovative Glasgow School of Art; and the attraction to the city of music and the fine arts – all have served to change the city's image and to place alongside its commercial and industrial base a rich cultural strand.

In some ways Glasgow has rediscovered its ancient cultural roots which are crystallized in the pinnacles of its magnificent gothic cathedral, built over the tomb of St Kentigern. Kentigern – or Mungo, as he came to be known (it is a familiar appellation of Latin-Welsh derivation, meaning 'dear friend') – is the patron and founder of Glasgow. Again, the classic Celtic missionary picture prevails. Mungo was the son of a British prince and a monk of the Irish tradition who was consecrated as the first bishop of the Strathclyde area, probably *c.* 543. He was caught up in the political disorder of the times, exiled to Cumbria later returning to Glasgow, to the monastery he founded. His tomb is reputed to be in the fan-vaulted crypt of the cathedral.

Little, other than legend, is known about Mungo. Even the outline above has been pieced together from fragmentary evidence. Nevertheless, the legends doubtless stretch back to a time when his memory was clearly hallowed and thus they give us clues to his character and mission. These legends are summed up in the schoolboy-like doggerel that was often used to sum up Glasgow's curious coat of arms:

The bell that never rang, the fish that never swam,
The tree that never grew, the bird that never flew.

The bell was part of Mungo's episcopal regalia, given at his ordination as a bishop. The fish is a salmon and relates to a legend about the King of Cadzaw. His wife had been unfaithful, and the King had taken a ring from the purse of the knight with whom she had been unfaithful and hurled it into the Clyde. On the promise of penance, the Queen asked for Mungo's help. He sent a monk to the Clyde, 'to angle with a hook, directing him to bring alive the first fish he might take, which being done the saint took from its mouth the ring and sent it to the Queen'.

The tree relates to another miracle attributed to Mungo, where he relit a twig which had been at the centre of an ever-burning holy fire. The bird was again at the centre of a miracle where Mungo restored it to life.

These legends suggest someone who was noted for his profound holiness and spiritual power. His missionary exploits are reflected in the motto which accompanies the coat of arms, deriving originally from an inscription on the bell in the Iron Church: 'Lord let Glasgow flourish through the preaching of the word and praising Thy name.' Certainly his austere and holy life is well attested to in the biographical fragments that are available to us. In the *Life* written by Jocelyn in about 1180, it is noted: 'Kentigern used to take ascetic cold baths, and afterwards he would sit to dry himself on the top of a hill called Gulath.'' Elsewhere it is recorded:

> They ... [were] accustomed to fasting and sacred vigils at certain seasons ... content with sparing diet and dress ... For, after the fashion of the Primitive Church under the apostles and their successors, possessing nothing of their own, and living soberly, righteously, and continently, they dwelt, as did Kentigern himself, in single cottages ...

Both the austere and holy life and the missionary impulse suggest, as later commentators have reflected, that Mungo kept a healthy balance and rhythm of the active and the contemplative. In this he echoes similar traditions to those that we discover in Cuthbert and Columbanus and in a number of other early Celtic missionaries. But one of the other strong emphases that is refracted through the lenses of legendary accounts is of Mungo's love of the natural world and of the animal kingdom. Here he also echoes emphases that are strongly resonant with the Celtic tradition as a whole. The arms of the city of Glasgow reflect such interests, and the translation of the city's name as 'Kentigern's beloved green place' further strengthens these associations. Mungo is part of that wider tradition which celebrates the integrity of God's creation by seeing the entire animate and inanimate world as part of one whole. This unified world is one in which we are stewards and also agents of God's creative and redemptive power.

The modern city of Glasgow, with its sharp contrasts, helps to earth these reflections in our contemporary world. The remnants of heavy industry and the fresher shoots of more modern 'high-tech' industries now stand alongside a thriving city of commerce. Glasgow itself sits in a bowl traversed by the River Clyde with the Scottish highlands rising to the north and other lower hills to the south. The Cathedral Church of St Mungo is still a dominant landmark. The world in which St Mungo ministered and set up his monastery remains visible, and the seeds of this ancient city have over the centuries given birth to a varied and mixed growth. Industry and commerce are now the fabric of the city. As such they do not stand as alien to the gospel which Mungo preached. Instead, that same gospel of creation and redemption, issuing from an integrated and living vision of God's purpose, offers a rich and essential foundation for our contemporary world. From whence does that foundation spring and what are its present implications?

CHRIST'S SINGLE BODY

In his correspondence with the Christian people of Corinth, St Paul is keen to stress the importance of unity with diversity. In his famous analogy which compares each of us to organs within a single body of the Church, Paul presses home the significance of the integrity of all God's people:

> Christ is like a single body with its many limbs and organs, which, many as they are, together make up one body; for in the one Spirit we were all brought into one body by baptism, whether Jews or Greeks, slave or free; we were all given that one Spirit to drink. (1 Corinthians 12:12–13)

Although the stress in this passage is on the unity and diversity of the Christian community, the implications run deeper still. Paul's embracing of Jew and Greek, slave and free, hints at that which is held in common within all humanity. A similar point is made in the Letter to the Galatians, and here male and female are also included. The references to the Gentiles and their

150

embracing of a natural law further strengthens a vision of one common humanity (Romans 2:12–16).

This emphasis upon wholeness, unity and a common purpose was not lost to the early missionaries within both Britain and Ireland, although the emphases within the Celtic and Roman traditions undoubtedly varied. Emphasis on the apostolic faith and the integrity of the gospel and its preaching was perhaps the single most significant strand in the Gregorian mission. Bede's *Ecclesiastical History* can be understood as a continuous commentary on the apostolic nature of the Church. This is manifested most clearly in his continued reference back to the divisions over the dating of Easter. Bede knew that the possibility of fragmentation within the Church was real. The preservation of apostolic continuity both in the faith and its transmission through the bishops of the Church remained an essential issue. Gregory was clear that in Britain, Augustine represented the Western Church and the Papacy. The principles set out by Gregory would guide Wilfrid and then Boniface in later generations in seeking unity in faith and in practice. By following such principles, the universal gospel of Jesus Christ, a gospel which itself promises wholeness through God's creativity and redeeming power, will be preached.

In the Celtic observance there was a greater concern for unity within what was effectively a European Church than is often realized. We have already encountered the patterns of dioceses existing to some degree both in Wales and in Ireland. Without a doubt, however, a rather different emphasis on integrity lay at the centre of the mission of the Celtic Christians. There was an all-embracing feel to the gospel message and the Christian life. There is a strong sense of all being part of one whole, without clear divisions between the sacred and the secular. As our reflections on Kentigern have suggested, there was also a sharp realization of the oneness of God's creation. The landscape in which people found themselves, the animal and plant kingdoms were an integrity. Finally, whilst we should not read into the Celtic traditions modern concepts of 'feminism' or the equality of the sexes, it is true that there was a greater equilibrium. The existence of double communities within the monastic life is one indicator, as is also the prominence of both lay women and women religious within the Celtic Church.

Bringing together the emphases of both the Roman and Celtic traditions offers a model which, even within the contemporary Church, has eluded us. Perhaps the Celtic search for integrity is most all-embracing. Within the broad understanding of wholeness are included a rich interweaving of creation and redemption which implies a commitment to redressing the inequalities within our world, working for a just and equitable peace and also taking seriously a ministry of healing. Healing has always been part of the reconciling ministry of Christ, but often in a less than balanced way. Fear of mortality, a philosophy of success and an overemphasis on highly technological approaches to illness has skewed our contemporary understanding of health. Health is now seen simply as the curing of or absence of illness. Where direct or complete cure is impossible, then more meagre resources are made available; the budgeting for geriatric and psychiatric medicine is correspondingly less than the budgeting for surgical and general medical treatment. Christian healing ministry itself is skewed by this and seen only as the 'curing' of life-threatening or debilitating illness.

Even in death the Celtic approach is broader. On Ninian's tomb, the epitaph ran:

At his most sacred tomb the sick are cured, the lepers cleansed, the wicked stricken with fear, the blind receive their sight; by all which the faith of the believer is confirmed ...

What was true of Ninian in death was true also of him in life, and we have already read of similar patterns in the life of Cuthbert, of Aidan, of Kentigern and others.

Seeing the entire creation within one compass offers a different set of criteria for making judgements about health and a healthy society. This is bound to lead to further presuppositions about the environment, about appropriate pressures within society, and about the nature of peace and justice. Where Christian people do become active in regard to the environment or matters of peace and justice, all too easily the approach is issue-based and divorced from theology and the gospel. The result is often a hortatory method which often descends into moralizing. The saints whose lives and teaching we have been reflecting upon throughout these chapters teach us otherwise. There is a marked emphasis on integrity and interdependence within God's creation.

As we saw in the previous chapter, the Roman missionaries' commitment to the unity of the apostolic faith has similarly eluded us, and fragmentation within the Christian Church mirrors fragmentation within contemporary society. Where moral imperatives are implied by the gospel, a divided Church undermines such teaching and fails to offer a prophetic and healing vision. Recovering these two traditions is an urgent priority. What more might we learn from the Celtic vision of an integrated and integrative creation? How might Kentigern, Cuthbert and Columbanus help us achieve a more unified world view?

GOD OF HEAVEN AND EARTH

The *Carmina Gadelica* offer numerous poems and prayers from the Celtic tradition which affirm the unity of God's creation. The individual and the community are both capable of seeing how everything within their experience is traceable to the Lord of all creation:

> Bless to me, O God, the moon that is above me,
> Bless to me, O God, the earth that is beneath me,
> Bless to me, O God, my wife and my children,
> And bless, O God, myself who have care of them;
> Bless to me my wife and my children,
> And bless, O God, myself who have care of them.[2]

In the traditions relating to St Patrick there is even material of a creed-like nature which brings together this sense of unity between God, humanity and the whole of creation.

> Our God, God of all men,
> God of heaven and earth, seas and rivers,
> God of sun and moon, of all the stars,
> God of high mountain and low valleys,
> God over heaven, and in heaven, and under heaven.
> He has a dwelling in heaven and earth and sea
> and in all things that are in them.[3]

One should, however, proceed with care in such reflection. In natural theology and indeed within religious traditions more generally, the celebration of God's responsibility and involvement in the natural world needs to be analysed with some clarity. As we have seen, Christian theology affirms both God's transcendence and immanence within creation. So, God is always ahead of us and beckoning us on. The imagery of the verses quoted reinforces this. God is the God of heaven and earth and of sun and moon. The expansive nature of these images reminds us of God's transcendence.

But the Christian tradition also stresses that God is immanent within creation. Humanity is capable of perceiving something of the nature and purposes of God through the created order. God is the God of seas and rivers, of high mountains and low valleys. 'He has a dwelling in heaven and earth and sea and in all things that are in them.'

There are dangers if God's immanence becomes total, for then God and creation become identical – we become pantheists. A journey down this particular path easily leads to a form of generalized 'nature mysticism'. This was encountered in some of the early Romantic poets, particularly in William Wordsworth. Some forms of 'New Age' thought have trodden this path and have sometimes drawn upon the early Celtic Christian traditions.

There is no clear evidence to suggest, however, that the Celtic embracing of one universe in God should lead us in the direction of pantheism. God is transcendent as well as being immanent in creation, and the redemption of the world is equally as important as the goodness of creation:

Thou loving Christ Who wast hanged upon the tree,
Each day and each night remember I Thy covenant;
In my lying down and rising up I yield me to Thy cross,
In my life and my death, my health thou art and my peace.

The presence of wayside crosses – perhaps the most common evidence of our Celtic Christian heritage – is a sharp reminder of the accent on redemption. But it is also salutary to remember that these crosses superimpose the sun upon the cross; it is that which gives them their distinctiveness. Christ is the great sun, but Christ is also Creator within the Holy Trinity of all things; the sun is one symbol of God's creation. God then is within his creation but never simply identified with it. In this the Celtic missionaries and contemplatives stand foursquare within the mainstream of Christian theology and spirituality. The created order is one means whereby we may perceive something of the nature and purposes of God. In this, the Celts drew upon the wellsprings of the Judaeo-Christian tradition. The Psalmist writes:

Bless the Lord, my soul.
Lord my God, you are very great,
clothed in majesty and splendour,
and enfolded in a robe of light.
You have spread out the heavens like a tent,
And laid the beams of your dwelling on the waters;
You take the clouds for your chariot,
riding on the wings of the wind. (Psalm 104:1–3)

In the gospels, too, Jesus refers to the natural world. Many of his parables and miracles are rooted in the world of vineyards and cornfields:

Think of the lilies: they neither spin nor weave; yet I tell you, even Solomon in all his splendour was not attired like one of them. If that is how God clothes the grass, which is growing in the field today, and tomorrow is thrown on the stove, how much more will he clothe you! (Luke 12:27–28)

The Celtic emphasis then on the integrity and interdependence of the universe, is built firmly upon the wider Christian tradition and it avoids the pitfalls of both pantheism and a God who is over-transcendent. God is discernible in all things, but not exhausted by them. God in Christ creates and redeems, and that too becomes transparent to us as we encounter the natural world.

> It is thou who makest the sun bright, together
> with the ice;
> It is thou who createst the rivers and the salmon
> all along the river.
> Though the children of Eve ill deserve the
> bird-flocks and the salmon,
> It was the Immortal One on the Cross who
> made both salmon and birds.

STILLING THE WAVES AND HEALING THE SICK

References to salmon and to birds and wild beasts are prolific in the Celtic sources. It was not only Kentigern who would commune with the animal kingdom. St Kevin, the seventh-century founder and first abbot of Glendalough, south-west of Dublin, is cared for by animals; it is said variously that either an otter or a badger brought him salmon daily. Otters also figured in Bede's *Life of Cuthbert*:

> The two otters bounded out of the water, stretched them-
> selves out before him, warmed his feet with their breath, and
> tried to dry him on their fur. They, having finished, received
> his blessing, and slipped back to their watery home.

This remarkable vision of wholeness is also associated with St Columbanus, who was surrounded by animals, much as the otters ministered to Cuthbert. It is important, however, to put this tradition in perspective, since this may help us both in understanding the context of the times but also in seeing if and how we might still learn from these narratives, poems and prayers. First of all, this embracing of nature is not unique to the Celtic or indeed Irish missionaries. It is rather in continuity with life in the earlier monastic communities; in that sense it is first and foremost an aspect of the monastic tradition. It is a tradition which is classically remembered too in the far later narratives relating to Francis of Assisi.

In seeing this as directly related to the monastic tradition, we can also see how it was bound up with the landscape and location within which the early monks and missionaries lived. The early Fathers including figures from the Egyptian and Palestinian deserts – Jerome, Anthony, Pachomius – were holy men who had left urban communities to live in lonely and often wild places. The company of animals is all that was available to them. Often as they told the story of the temptations that they experienced in the desert, the imagery used was one which drew from the habits and behaviour of wild animals. The demons who tempted them took on the form of wild beasts. This was equally true for the Irish and other Celtic monks. Often the places where the monasteries were situated were lonely and exposed. Even where communities grew up around an oratory, still the monastery would be away from urban centres; this was part of the nature of the Irish landscape. Tiny islands in the Atlantic, Lindisfarne, Inner Farne, Glendalough and Ciaran's (Kieran) monastery on the Shannon at Clonmacnoise were all isolated places. Even Kentigern's foundation in Glasgow should not be seen in the context of a modern urban centre. It was a new monastery set within a bowl in the wild Scottish hills.

This reminds us that the Celtic 'integrated view of God's creation' should not be seen in modern terms. The monks whose exploits we have encountered were exposed to the full splendours of nature. Celebration of God's creation was naturally provoked by the immediacy of a wild natural environment; it was the only world they had on which to reflect. They were dependent upon it and upon the other creatures with whom they found themselves in company. For these reasons it was essential and even instinctual that their existence and the landscape in which they were set should be taken together and offered to God in celebration, in thanksgiving. Such an appreciation helps us better understand the significance of miracles in the accounts of Bede and others. Everyone was both dependent upon and at the mercy of the elements, the wild animals and the landscape in which they lived. Miracles abound in these accounts and testify to the faithfulness of God in what was often a very dangerous world. St Aidan's blessing upon some seafarers is a classic example:

> When Aidan had blessed them and commended them to God, he gave them some holy oil, saying: 'When you set sail, you will encounter a storm and contrary winds. Remember then to pour the oil that I am giving you on the sea, and the wind will immediately drop, giving you a pleasant, calm voyage and a safe return home.' Everything happened as the bishop foretold.

There is no doubt that there was an integrated view of the natural world, the animal kingdom, human experience and God's providence. Such an integrated view was provoked by the pattern of life at the time. It was a pattern which also integrated disease, injury and miraculous cure with God's providential dealings. Healing was not somehow separated off into a discrete world of sacramental theology. Nor, of course, was there a developed realm of professional medicine, even in the way in which that might have developed in the more urban existence of either ancient Greece or in the Roman Empire. The Celtic world was a world exposed to nature in a manner to which even the term rural hardly does justice. Healing is all of a piece with the world we have described. Bede's *Life of Cuthbert* recounts one miracle after another and Eddius' *Life of Wilfrid* is similarly studded with miraculous healings. So Bede recounts an incident where Cuthbert encounters a girl with serious neck pains:

'One of [the nuns] ... was seriously ill, seized with pains in the head and all down one side ... Cuthbert's companions pointed this out to him and begged him to heal her. Full of pity for her wretchedness he anointed her with holy oil. She began to improve from that very moment and in a few days completely recovered.'

This incident is one of five which follow one after the other in Bede's *Life*. We have already seen how Ninian's tomb retained healing powers, even after the saint's death. The wooden buttress of the Church against which Aidan leaned as he died was imbued with similar properties. Despite fires which destroyed the church, the beam survived:

Since that day many are known to have obtained the grace of healing at this spot, and many have cut chips of wood from the beam and put them in water, by which means many have been cured of their diseases.

SEEKING INTEGRITY AGAIN

The world which we have encountered in these past few pages is an irrecoverable world. It is bathed in an attractive romance and echoes of it can be recaptured in some of the lonely places inhabited by the holy people in an antique world. The precise vision is irrecoverable, however, for more than one reason. Perhaps the most critical issue is the contemporary environment in which we find ourselves. Scotland, Wales, Ireland and England are now thoroughly urbanized. In those places where the remnants of the rural idyll are still cultivated the urban and the technological still invade. Even the quietest hedgerow and the deepest copse is now no longer immune to the advances of the mobile phone. The pollution and waste caused by great cities is often deposited upon some of the quietest and most rural backwaters of these islands. Norway, it is said, suffers seriously from the acid rain produced by the mammoth power stations at Ferrybridge, Eggborough and Drax in the southern part of Yorkshire. Ireland, which retains a greater hold on its countryside than the other three nations, is inextricably caught up in the industrialization and urbanization of Western Europe. This process is increasingly unavoidable as developed and developing nations become ever more interdependent through the complexities of a global economy.

This process also means that by far the majority of people in our four countries now live in cities. Life in cities is in almost complete contrast to the world of Aidan and Cuthbert, Dewi and Ciaran, Mungo and Patrick. In large areas of urban Britain, for example, open space is at a premium and the natural world far from obvious. Journeys through London's docklands, through the heart of Glasgow, or south from Jordanstown on the Belfast urban motorway towards Armagh confront the traveller with concrete and brick and huge concentrations of commercial and industrial buildings. In an earlier chapter we stumbled upon the urban farm in London's Vauxhall; a miniature farm which has been artificially imported into the inner city to offer young people some experience of a more rural and, in one sense, a more natural world. Such developments point up the stark differences between contemporary city life and early medieval monastic patterns of living in community. Cities are fragmented, but more than that they are far removed from nature. It is impossible to appreciate the integrity of God's creation as a natural daily matter of fact as the Celtic missionaries and mystics did.

For that reason it is both inappropriate and indeed impossible to recover the precise vision of integrity that was the property of that early-medieval world. Our concerns are different. We seek integrity in creation because the world has been plundered and abused. Human survival itself seems threatened by pollution and by the abuse of the environment. The integrity that Columbanus and others perceived is no longer an option. Nevertheless, the ability to see our existence, however different it may be from theirs, as part of one whole within God's providence remains essential. In other words, the ultimate vision is one which we can still share with them. The landscape and the understanding of the world offered to us by science will be different. If Christian theology and spirituality is to make sense of our contemporary world, then it must take these profoundly different contingent facts seriously.

Some examples may assist us in appreciating this. Although the vast majority of us no longer live in such close proximity to the natural world and thus feel ourselves less directly dependent upon the landscape, the elements and the animal kingdom, we have already discovered how essentially interdependent different nations are within the world economy. Inflation in developed countries, and third world debt bear directly upon each other. Policies relating to import tariffs and to the subsidizing of inefficient industries within developed nations have immediate mutual effects in the world of international trade. This is not, however, the way that it is generally seen either politically or theologically. Nations still act out of their own interests, rarely seeing that somewhere down the line even self-interest may rebound upon them. Developing nations and the developed world both suffer.

Theology has failed to take sufficient account of the autonomy of economics and of the expertise required in this area of human endeavour. The result is that social issues are often divorced both from empirical facts and from a theological base. To approach such issues in a vacuum from a clear and integrated theological analysis will produce a purely 'issue-based' approach which often degenerates into sloganism. Theological integrity is an essential tool in the contemporary analysis.

Similar points can be made about that other aspect of wholeness relating to healing of the mind, body and spirit. The miraculous world of Cuthbert and Kentigern is not a world we can recover. But health as a concept needs to be recovered in its fullness. It needs to relate to wholeness and a manner of life which nurtures human flourishing and fulfilment. Such an approach will take medical science seriously, and not see high-cost, 'high tech' medicine as effectively the core and apogee of health care. Those things in our world which alienate human beings from each other – which cause impossible stress, and which deny the spiritual – need to be identified so that a holistic view of health might be recovered. The Christian sacramental tradition in relation to healing is part of but not a substitute for an integrative vision of health within the community. The Celtic missionaries were right in seeing healing as part of a much wider integrity within creation. That once again is a salutary lesson that we still must learn.

Finally, and this relates both to economics and the earlier reflections on fragmentation in the inner city, care for the poor is part of this same vision that sees God's creation as one integrated whole. In speaking of the local and the universal, we encountered the fragmentation of communities. This is another aspect of that same phenomenon which requires us to see the world as all part of one economy. Without denying people free will, we must accept that we are interdependent within our own communities. The misery caused by unemployment presses this home to us perhaps more sharply than anything else. No politicians have yet been prepared to admit openly that full employment is now a chimera. We shall never recover it again. Facing that truth with realism reminds us that if there are insufficient jobs to go round, then there will always be 'victims' within our society. A 'privatized' view of moral and social policy, where all individuals must fight their own corner to survive, is not simply inadequate, it is manifestly untrue. However hard everyone works, the economic realities cannot provide sufficient jobs for all. Interdependence within an integrated creation offers a different vision where even though jobs may not be available for all, everyone will have a part to play in the wider community where cultural, spiritual and moral values remain paramount.

This suggests a radical reappraisal of economic and social priorities. It assumes that humanity works interdependently and co-operatively and that individuals and communities act as agents of God's creative and redemptive power. God is already in the world, working through individuals and through common grace. Esther de Waal writes: 'A world made whole; a world in which the divides go down, and the barriers are crossed, becomes a world which integrates and heals'.⁵ That is the vision offered by Christ's gospel of reconciliation. 'God was in Christ reconciling the world to himself' (2 Corinthians 5:19). It was a world that the Celtic Christians brought sharply into focus. We cannot precisely recover their world, nor should we attempt to replicate their exact patterns of life and theological reflection, but their ultimate vision of a world caught up into the Trinitarian life of God should certainly be ours too.

Prayer

O Lord God, grant that after the pattern of
the life of blessed Ninian you will give us
humility and wisdom, justice, kindness and virtue.
May we offer refreshment to all who come to us,
A roof for the destitute and comfort for captives;
Bread for the hungry, and sweet draughts of refreshment
   to those who thirst;
Protection to the orphan and widow, and support
   for the poor;
Grant this in the name of Our Lord and Saviour
Jesus Christ, in whose service blessed Ninian both
   lived and died.

Amen.

Based upon a eulogy on the death of St Ninian

UNCEASING PRAYER

Prayer is the essential basis of all Christian life and mission. This is the testimony of both the Roman and Celtic missionaries to these lands.

Clonmacnoise is literally at the heart of Ireland. Situated on a gravel ridge within an enormous meander of the River Shannon it is a place of incomparable beauty, peace and tranquillity. The circular towers, the impressive ruined temples and the stunning remains of the great castle fortress make Clonmacnoise a particularly evocative Celtic site. It was here in or around the year 544 that St Ciaran founded what was to become one of the most important monastic centres in Ireland, second only to Armagh. Clearly Ciaran knew what he was searching for, for the contemporary tranquillity of this holy place almost certainly resembles closely the site as Ciaran found it, and before the more extensive monastic buildings were established. Later, between AD 700 and AD 1200, the monastery would form the focus for a major centre of piety, learning, trade and craftsmanship. It became part of a larger urban settlement. Placed at the crossing of two great routes, the river running north/south and the main cross-country road running east/west.

This interesting series of contrasts between silence and busyness, worldly life and isolation sets the scene well for the place of prayer within the Christian life. For, although monastic foundations are often sited in remote and sometimes wild places, still the life of prayer must in a variety of different ways engage with the things of the world. Even contemplatives and hermits are keen to relate their intercession to the world within which they are set.

Ciaran and Clonmacnoise pick up strands that are resonant within the Celtic roots of Irish and British Christianity. Rather unusually for a Celtic missionary, Ciaran was not from a high family. Born in *c.* 512, he was the son of a travelling carpenter from Connaught; his family could trace back their roots to a pre-Celtic descent. Ciaran became a disciple of St Enda on the Aran Isles, to the west of Ireland. Gradually he made his way westwards and founded Clonmacnoise, only a year before he died.

As with many other Celtic saints, numerous legends and fables survived. In the case of Ciaran they testify to his remarkable religious spirit which was founded upon a profound and rigorous pattern of prayer. Indeed, one monastic foundation was so alarmed by his holiness and charity that the brothers remonstrated with him: 'Go away for we cannot suffer you here with us.'

Undoubtedly, Ciaran and his community at Clonmacnoise were assisted in the life of prayer by the beauty of the natural environment in which they found themselves. His experience, even though it is now sparsely documented, is sufficient to give us clues to the emphases and strengths of early Celtic spirituality. As always the natural environment is important; *place* is of crucial significance to the early traditions within Britain and Ireland and most particularly for Celtic Christians. The situation at Clonmacnoise is of a piece with this, for the material world in which people found themselves was of seminal importance in transforming Clonmacnoise from a silent and tranquil place into a centre of great commerce by the early medieval period. This placed before those who lived there in community a tension between retreat from, and an embracing of the material world. This tension remains within the Christian tradition, although the Judaeo-Christian pattern generally has been one of embracing the world. As the writer of Genesis noted: 'God saw all that he had made, and it was very good' (Genesis 1:31). Creation is affirmed. Celtic prayers from the Outer Hebrides continue to reflect the goodness of God's creation:

There is no plant in the ground,
But it is full of His virtue,
There is no form in the strand,
But it is full of His blessing ...

There is no bird on the wing,
There is no star in the sky,
There is nothing beneath the sun,
But proclaims his goodness.[1]

This embracing of the natural world was essential to the monastic life. Ciaran, dying so young in his beloved Clonmacnoise, did so staring up into the wide blue heavens, and within the rich green of the grassy meadows which are virtually encircled by the slow creeping of the great Shannon to its estuary in the west of Ireland. Hermits were able to take advantage of this outstanding natural beauty and to experience a unity with God's creation with great power and clarity. An eighth-century Irish writer puts it thus:

Alone in my little hut without a human being in my company dear has been the pilgrimage before going to meet death.

A remote hidden little cabin,
for forgiveness of my sins;
a conscience upright and spotless
before holy Heaven.

It is difficult to imagine lines that could more effectively capture the story of Ciaran. The integration of Ciaran and others with the natural world in which they lived was not some ancient form of conservation awareness; instead it was merely a reflection of their continuous contact with nature throughout their daily life. We referred earlier to the ease with which modern civilization is either alienated from or at least distanced from the natural world by life in cities; the natural world, as Ciaran, Cuthbert and Columba knew it, is simply not obvious within contemporary conurbations. On Iona, on Lindisfarne, or at Clonmacnoise, one can still recapture the immediacy of the natural world which provoked patterns of prayer such as those illustrated above. It is easy to exaggerate the degree of 'retreat' exercised in the Celtic monastic tradition. Certainly in Ireland, much of Scotland and in Northumbria, peaceful, lonely and wild locations were part of everyday experience.

None of this denies the characteristic nature of Celtic spirituality; indeed it tends to underline its individuality. As we have hinted in earlier chapters, the environment, the historical patterns which developed, and in this case the natural world help to shape Christianity in any place and in any age. During the early period of Christian mission in these islands, the immediacy of God's presence in creation, and also the cruelty, power and sheer force of the natural world are manifested both in prayer and elsewhere in the Christian tradition. 'St Patrick's Breastplate' captures this vividly, and the stories of the missionary travels of Columba, Aidan and Cuthbert strongly suggest the same. Nature was then, as it is now, 'red in tooth and claw'. Often prayer and devotion would be practised almost in spite of, or in the face of the unfriendly elements and terrain. But whatever the difficulties and threats, prayer remained the priority, and the foundation of the life of the early monks and missionaries from both the Celtic and Roman traditions.

MONASTIC PRAYER

In the Eastern so-called 'hesychastic' tradition of prayer, the central assumption is that through the stilling of the heart and mind each of us is capable of moving towards union with God. In Orthodox spirituality and theology this process is sometimes called *theiosis* or 'deification'; humanity becomes increasingly 'divinized'. The route to such a union with God is via total commitment to the holy life and what St Paul refers to as unceasing prayer. Paul writes in 1 Thessalonians 5:16–18, 'Rejoice evermore. Pray without ceasing. In everything give thanks: for this is the will of God in Christ Jesus concerning you.' This same pattern has been reflected in popular devotional works like *The Way of the Pilgrim,* which encourage the Christian soul to use rhythmically and repetitively the 'Jesus Prayer' in a manner which eventually becomes 'unceasing'. Similar patterns of rhythmic prayer exist also within the Western tradition based upon the Rosary or, following the Franciscan method, using brief repeated formulae – perhaps the *Gloria Patri* or 'My God and My All'.

Such patterns of prayer reflect the desire to attune the heart and mind of each individual Christian soul to the things of God. Often posture and breathing patterns are taken into account such that the rhythm of life effectively seeks to resonate to the 'heartbeat of God'. It is an attempt to weave together the life of humanity and God into one tapestry or seamless robe.

But alongside this, the Christian faith has always been affirmed and practised within the community and not purely within the lives of individuals. At the heart of the monastic life lies the attempt to weave a pattern of unceasing prayer into the life of the religious community. It is a tradition which takes time and sanctifies it. The day is punctuated with regular times of prayer. This pattern is not unique to Christianity; Muslims pray at regular points throughout the day. The Christian patterns of daily prayer stretch back into the wider context of the Judaeo-Christian tradition and can be identified well before the advent of Jesus' ministry. So, in the book of Daniel, the writer notes: '[Daniel] had had windows made in his roof-chamber looking towards Jerusalem; and there he knelt down three times a day and offered prayers and praises to his God as his custom had always been' (Daniel 6:10).

The early Christian monasteries built upon this practice and a pattern emerged whereby each day was sanctified by a regular round of prayer. It was this pattern that would later develop, assisted by the Rule of St Benedict and other later monastic observances, into the 'hours of prayer'. In many traditions even the night was punctuated with offices – Compline, Vigils, Lauds and Prime. Matins and Evensong (or Vespers) often became major offices and the little hours of Terce, Sext and None (said at the third, sixth and ninth hours: 9 a.m., 12 noon, 3 p.m.) punctuated the day. This pattern would then stand alongside the daily community mass or eucharist. A similar structure, albeit somewhat simplified, exists in Monastic communities still. Within Anglicanism the pattern of Morning and Evening Prayer (Matins and Evensong) is still required of all clergy. The Anglican practice is a simplified form of the office devised by Thomas Cranmer to encourage laity to structure their daily lives according to a regular pattern of prayer.

The early missionaries were no strangers to this commitment to unceasing prayer. Bede writes of St Cuthbert:

> Above all else, he was afire with heavenly love, unassumingly patient, devoted to unceasing prayer, and kindly to all who came to him for comfort. He regarded as equivalent to prayer the labour of helping the weaker brethren with advice, remembering that he who said, '*Thou shalt love the Lord thy God*,' also said, '*love thy neighbour*.'

The traditions relating to St Cuthbert all bear out this witness of Bede. Elsewhere, both in the *Ecclesiastical History* and in Bede's *Life of Cuthbert*, there are testimonies to the rigorous life led by the saint. There are also stories reflecting Cuthbert's confidence in the power of intercessory prayer and thus in the continuing providence of God. The tradition of Cuthbert's time as a hermit reinforces this further; the existence of oratories at Lindisfarne, both in the Priory and on St Cuthbert's Island (just off Holy Island), and on the Farnes suggests that Cuthbert's missionary and episcopal work issued from a life of committed prayer and contemplation. The establishment, in 1987, of a hermitage and contemplative house at Shepherd's Law dedicated to St Mary and St Cuthbert reflects the fact that Cuthbert's life was rooted in prayer. The stories that we have already encountered of Cuthbert show that similar expressions of God's presence within creation as were there with Ciaran are a central part of the Northumbrian Celtic tradition.

Once again a romantic revival of Celtic Christianity in Britain and Ireland can easily drive a wedge between the Irish and Roman roots of our tradition. A Celtic revival was overdue and has reminded us of the significance of this part of our heritage. It has reminded us too of the essential part played by local traditions. It is easily extended, however, into a naïve contrast even in this realm of spirituality and prayer. The fundamental significance of prayer was not absent in the Roman tradition. Indeed it was again at the heart of the Christian life. As we discovered earlier, Gregory the Great was reluctant to abandon the contemplative life for the more worldly responsibilities forced upon him when he became Pope. In reflecting on the death of Pope Gregory, Bede quotes conversations between the pontiff and his deacon, Peter:

> Gregory described his former spiritual state, then sadly continued: 'My pastoral responsibilities now compel me to have dealings with worldly men, and after the unclouded beauty of my former peace, it seems that my mind is bespattered with the mire of daily affairs. For when it has squandered itself in attention to the worldly affairs of numberless people, even though it turns inward again to meditate on spiritual things, it does so with unmistakably lessened powers.'

Bede's account should not be taken to imply a despising of the pastoral ministry or of matters of the world. Gregory was the model of a good pastor and an outstanding ecclesiastical statesman. Instead, the words imply the need to integrate the daily affairs of the world with the fundamental life of contemplative prayer. Gregory was clear what God had called him to do, and his pontificate was rooted in his life as a monk. Significantly it was a monk, indeed the prior of Gregory's own Benedictine monastery on the Celian Hill in Rome whom he would choose and send to be the apostolic missionary to England. Augustine was thus also rooted in the community life of contemplative prayer and his band of missionaries set up a new monastery as the basis of the Roman mission; a Benedictine house was established in Canterbury which would be the foundation of the great cathedral that we know today. As we shall see in our final chapter, the influence of Benedict within the whole of western Europe was to be seminal.

The conclusion is, then, not that the Celtic and Roman missionaries prayed identically or indeed that the patterns of mission were precisely the same. Instead one can affirm the essential role played by the different monastic observances in the process of evangelization. We can see furthermore how that monastic foundation inevitably required both missionary work and the nurture of daily Christian life to spring from the deep wells of contemplative prayer.

CELTIC RHYTHMS

The contrast is perhaps most obviously identified through the rhythmic repetitive style of much Celtic prayer. Such repetition may refer to a theological principle, for example, the Trinity – petitions are made in a threefold litany-like pattern. Repetition may also refer to the natural creation or to members of the family or others included within the prayer, each requiring similar rhythms to be repeated throughout the devotion.

These rhythmic compositions are often gleaned from the *Carmina Gadelica*, collected by Carmichael in the latter part of the nineteenth century. These resonant patterns, however, have been transmitted from generation to generation orally and it is likely that they represent characteristic structures and rhythms which derive from early Gaelic/Celtic/Irish culture. Similar patterns and even themes (particularly relating to the created order) go back into the pre-Christian era. The ancient themes of light and darkness, and of protecting against the evil one, are seen clearly in this devotion from Mary Macrae, a dairy-woman in Harris:

God with me lying down
God with me rising up;

God with me in each ray of light,
Nor I a ray of joy without him,
    Nor one ray without him

God with me protecting,
The Lord with me directing,
The Spirit with me strengthening,
    For ever and for evermore,

    Ever and evermore, Amen.
    Chief of chiefs, Amen.[2]

In the second double-stanza here we also encounter the Trinitarian focus to which we shall return. The devotional rhythms established in this tradition richly enhanced both worship through their poetry and also private prayer through their repetitive and simple structures. Modern writers of prayers have understandably and profitably built upon this tradition.[3]

Perhaps the theme which remains most characteristic of Celtic prayer and spirituality is that of creation. The closeness of the natural world and the sense of dependence upon it made it the focus of prayers of thanksgiving, invocation and blessing. Two rather different examples serve to press home the point:

Be blessing, O God, my little cow,
    And be blessing, O God, my intent;
O God my partnership blessing thou,
    And my hands that to milking are sent.

This, and the devotion that follows, are both traditional Gaelic poems, collected by Carmichael:

> Thou King of the moon and of the sun,
>   Of the stars thou loved and fragrant King,
> Thou thyself knowest our needs each one,
>   O merciful God of everything.[4]

There is good evidence to show that the integrity of life in relation to the natural creation (including the elements) is part of a long tradition stretching back to the seventh century and indeed beyond that into pagan Celtic culture. Tales of the miracles of Cuthbert, Aidan and Brendan are directly related to their prayers aimed at taming the elements. Bede's story of Aidan's rescuing of the royal city (presumably Ad Gefrin – modern-day Yeavering) from fire is a good example:

> Directly the wind became favourable he [Penda – the pagan King of Mercia] set fire to this mass, intending to destroy the city ... When the saint [Aidan] saw the column of smoke and flame wafted by the winds above the city walls, he is said to have raised his eyes and hands to heaven, saying with tears: 'Lord, see what evil Penda does!' No sooner had he spoken than the wind shifted away from the city, and drove back the flames on to those who had kindled them, so injuring some and unnerving all that they abandoned their assault on a city so clearly under God's protection.

This invocation of God's grace for protection and salvation is the essence of the so-called 'breastplate prayers', of which 'St Patrick's Breastplate' is the most well known. Once again there is a repetition which is the mark of a litany-style devotion. Such patterns were repeated and developed, during Anglo-Saxon times, in the collections of Latin prayers for private use. The most famous examples of such collections are the *Book of Cerne* and the *Book of Nunnaminster*. Although the *Book of Cerne* is Mercian, of the ninth century, it is certain that the prayers there collected are much older, and there are strong Irish traits in these collected devotions. The breastplate prayers recur here too:

> Guard my mouth lest I speak vain things and tell profane tales
> Guard my eyes lest they look upon a woman with
>   lustful desire
> Guard my ears lest they listen to detraction or the idle
>   words of liars
> Guard my feet lest they frequent the houses of leisure
> Guard my hands lest they stretch out often for gifts.

Precisely the same litany patterns that we have encountered in the Hebridean prayers of the *Carmina Gadelica* are there.

Within these books are collected another group of prayers which are also common in the Celtic tradition, namely those which have an ascetic and penitential content. Darkness and light remain important and derive from pre-Christian themes. The significance of human sinfulness is essential to Celtic spirituality. Again we see it clearly in the *Book of Cerne*. In this example the flavour is almost over-rich:

> By your loins which were always filled with divine virtue,
>   renew in my loins the spirit of holiness.
> By your most chaste head, O Christ, have mercy on my
>   wicked head.
> By your blessed eyes, spare my polluted eyes ...

This preoccupation with penance and asceticism is central to the Irish tradition. Indeed, the early monasteries of Ireland were important centres of penance both for lay people and for the religious. The tradition of the 'soul-friend' or *anmchara* comes from this source, and offers a flexible pattern of spiritual direction; the Celtic idea of the soul-friend has complemented the Latin pattern. There is a well-known saying, often attributed to St Brigid, that 'anyone without a soul-friend is like a body without a head'. Lay men and women were as likely to have soul-friends as were priests and monks. Although the penitential discipline stemming from the Irish monasteries was rigorous, it did not lack generosity or breadth. The notion of a soul-friend supports this. Penance was seen effectively as healing, as a cure for sin.

Alongside this understanding and even gentle approach to penance stand also the lyrical litanies to the Holy Trinity. Many of these that are well-known are again collected in the *Carmina Gadelica* :

The blessing of God be upon you, that good may come to you;
The blessing of Christ be upon you, that good be done to you;
The blessing of the Holy Ghost be yours, that good be the
    course of your life,
each day of your arising, each night of your lying down,
for evermore, Amen.

The structure of Celtic prayer reflects a profound rootedness in Trinitarian theology. Esther de Waal points out that the Celtic tradition, as it has been transmitted over the centuries in the Hebrides, clearly sets life in the context of the Trinity. At birth, each child was sprinkled by the midwife with three drops of water on its forehead in the name of the Trinity. The mother would then quietly say:

> The blessing of the Holy Three
> Little love, be dower to thee,
> Wisdom, peace and purity.

Invocation of the Trinity would not begin and end there. It would continue such that throughout life the Trinitarian God would be called upon to offer the gifts appropriate to that moment. Similarly it would underpin daily prayer and the desire for God to sanctify and protect each individual and the entire community throughout the day and night:

> The God of life with guarding hold you,
> The loving Christ with guarding fold you,
> The Holy Spirit, guarding, mould you,
> each night of life to aid, enfold you,
> each day and night of life uphold you.

The social implications of Trinitarian doctrine would have made great sense in a rural society where relationships were mainly within the family and small groups. Irish Christianity in the early centuries was of just this character. The great breastplate of St Patrick is punctuated by appeals to the Trinitarian God:

> I bind unto myself today
> The strong name of the Trinity:
> By invocation of the same,
> The Three in One and One in Three.

The prayer for protection and the invocation of the Trinity become one and the same thing. The same was true of healing and of the blessings which accompanied it:

In the eye of God,
In the love of Jesus,
In the name of the Spirit,
The Trinity of power.

The devotions focused upon here make clear something of the atmosphere and character of prayer in the Celtic tradition. The integrity of that tradition is clear. It issues from a close relationship with the natural order and thus also with the elements. It invokes God's protection and assistance when the natural world feels hostile or dangerous. It reminds humanity of its frailty and its need for healing and repentance. It offers reassurance in the profoundly Trinitarian basis of prayer and in layer upon layer of litanies, rather as in the Orthodox tradition. All of this suggests an interrelationship between God, the creation and humanity which can be likened to a complex woven tapestry. It is a tapestry which is not vulnerable to one stitch being cut and the entire fabric fragmenting. The repetition itself holds together the weave ever more closely.

CONTEMPLATION AND ACTIVITY

Reflection upon the integrity of Celtic prayer highlights the holding together of the life of prayer, and the active life of Christian mission and discipleship. The earthiness of the Irish and Hebridean prayers leaves us in no doubt about the interconnectedness of the active and contemplative life within Christianity. Our glances at the ministry of Gregory the Great have equally convinced us of his commitment to holding together this tension. But it is not only the corporate monastic life which testifies to the importance of prayer in the work of the early missionaries. The stricter, more ascetic approach to contemplative prayer was present in the numerous hermits and hermitages known to exist from the early period. In Ireland, the hermit life was of particular significance. In Northumbria, the sites of numerous hermitages are still known. Taking its cue from the tradition of the Egyptian and Palestinian Desert Fathers, the hermit life would later make a still more significant contribution to Christian mission. Even as active a missioner as St Francis of Assisi is known for his commitment to contemplative prayer. This is testified to in the hermitages set up by him in the Italian Appennines at La Verna, Spoleto, and outside Assisi itself.

To live the life of a hermit was not necessarily a permanent vocation. Cuthbert spent times in isolation in between periods of concentrated mission. Sometimes even involuntary isolation would prove to be an opportunity for strengthening the missionary impulse that would follow. In his *Life of Wilfrid*, Eddius describes just one such occasion:

> Wilfrid was hidden away, under guard, in a place which was rarely brightened by the sun during the day and where no lamp was lighted to grace the hours of the night. His guardians hearing him continually singing psalms, looked into the cell and found the darkness of the night turned into day. Thunderstruck themselves, they terrified others with the tale of his holiness.

Eddius describes how, during Wilfrid's imprisonment, the King offered preferment and material riches if he would forsake the commands of Rome for the ordinances of the King. Wilfrid remained steadfast in adhering to the Holy See, however, and Eddius is so moved as to burst into spontaneous prayer as he tells the tale:

O Christ, Eternal light, who dost not absent those who acknowledge Thee, Thou whom we believe to be the true light illuminating 'every man that cometh into this world'.

This story is paralleled to some degree, in the story told by Adamnan, Columba's biographer. Columba retired to a lonely island to live there for three days and nights without food or drink. At night a remarkable light burned its way out of the cell through the keyhole. This was similar to the light which engulfed Wilfrid in his prison cell. Both tales press home effectively the esteem with which the life of contemplation, and the role of hermits was viewed. But both tales also relate to the life of two of the most active and effective missionaries of the early period. Contemplation and activity were symbiotic; they fed on each other and nourished each other.

The missionary lives of the saints was unthinkable and unsustainable without the underlying commitment to the life of prayer. The building of the new Benedictine monasteries at Ripon and at Hexham was part of Wilfrid's strategy as an evangelist. In developing the life of these foundations he was clear that he was establishing effective missionary bases for future generations. In doing so he was also founding rich cultural centres which would shape an emerging nation 'in the Christian life'. The monasteries would become centres of learning and of the arts, and the Benedictine inheritance in particular would be one of the crucial factors in the building of European culture. The Celtic monastic inheritance, albeit with different structures and patterns of prayer, would perform a similar function in Ireland, in Wales, in Cornwall and later in Scotland, Northumbria and East Anglia. Commitment to prayer automatically brought with it a missionary bias. The mission of the Church was unsustainable apart from the life of the monasteries and periods of withdrawal and contemplation.

SUSTAINING THE CHRISTIAN LIFE

The pattern that has just been described – effectively an oscillation between contemplation and activity – seems obvious enough in retrospect. The Old Testament tradition, as we saw, included patterns of daily prayer. The Essenes, the ascetic community thought to have inhabited buildings close to the caves where the Dead Sea Scrolls were discovered, lived a lonely and rigorous life not unlike that of later Christian monks. The Desert Fathers and the later patterns of monastic life developing from them (differently in the Christian East and West) owed much to the Judaic tradition, but still brought the fresh insights of the Christian gospel to bear. Following the conversion of Constantine and the later development of Christendom, the life lived and taught by the early missionaries in Britain and Ireland became the standard by which true Christian discipleship could be measured. Humanity's creation and redemption by God were part of the immediate world within which people lived and breathed. God's presence, providence and judgement had real implications for people's daily life. High mortality rates meant that chantries and masses for the dead also became part of the fabric of everyday life and death. Viewed under the providence of God, death was a very serious matter in the economy of salvation.

It is less easy to view things in this way in our contemporary world. We no longer live cheek by jowl with the natural order as did the Irish Christians of the fifth, sixth and seventh centuries; the majority of us live in cities or semi-urban contexts. Secondly, the advent of critical scholarship has produced a more sceptical frame of mind in the Western world. Finally, a market-based consumer materialism has radically affected our hierarchy of values. Even those stories from Bede which are less exotically miraculous strike the modern mind as somewhat quaint. It is instead his ability to catalogue, with an amazing degree of accuracy, the historical developments of the late sixth, seventh and early eighth centuries in England which continues to impress the modern mind. Under such conditions, it is less easy to see the primary significance of prayer and to hold in tension contemplation and activity.

Even before moving on to the necessary tension between contemplative prayer and the active Christian life, it is essential to establish the priority of prayer and worship. Earlier this century, Kenneth Kirk, in his classic *The Vision of God*, argued that the Christian life must begin with worship and prayer.

> Before the earliest Gospel assumed its present shape, the church had fixed on the Transfiguration as the central moment of the Lord's earthly life. It had surrounded that moment with a glamour and allusion and allegorism so complex that it cannot now with any certainty be analysed into its constituent elements. And it had done this as though to remind itself that the whole Gospel, from beginning to end, must be read and regarded as one great vision of God in Christ, akin to the vision given to the favoured three on the Mount of Transfiguration.

Kirk's point was not that humanity should seek after overwhelming mystical experience. That was not what he meant by the vision of God. Instead he believed, it is by fixing our eyes, in steady gaze, through worship and prayer upon the God who is revealed in Jesus Christ that we shall be transformed by that vision of God:

> What Christianity offers, with its fellowship and sacraments, its life of prayer and service, its preaching of the Incarnate Son of God, is the same vision in ever-increasing plenitude ...

There is no need to ask whether we are psychologically capable of seeing God; we have already seen him.[5]

Following Kirk's account, all Christian experience and reflection becomes one. Theology is not divided into discrete disciplines. For faith is rooted in prayer and worship and these shape our belief and orientate our lives. Morality becomes not an impossible exercise of the will, of pulling oneself up by one's own bootstraps. Instead, life lived with our eyes fixed upon God will be transformed. To pray regularly, then, actually affects our quality of life. It helps shape our response within the gospel. Kirk is not the only writer to argue for the profound effect of a life rooted in worship and contemplative prayer. Iris Murdoch, the novelist and philosopher, herself an agnostic, commends prayer for similar reasons. It has, she argues, the effect of 'unselfing' both individuals and communities. She gives the interesting example of someone working at their desk and feeling profoundly 'at odds with the world and with her fellow human beings'. Suddenly her eye alights upon a kestrel hovering. The wonder of this experience momentarily 'unselfs' her and when she returns to her work much of the anger, tension and self-absorption have been released.

The Christian soul will want to press this still further. This is precisely what Kirk does. He makes it clear that Christian life and mission are both essential to each other. But he also makes it clear that contemplative prayer and corporate worship are the foundations of all Christian life. Commitment to these will establish Christian discipleship, rooted in the vision of God. This is the same belief as that affirmed by the earliest missionaries to these islands from both the Irish and Roman traditions. It is the same transforming vision given expression in some of the incomparable Celtic prayers and devotions of that period and through to the present day.

Prayer

God to enfold,
God to surround,
God in speech-told,
God my thought-bound.

God when I sleep,
God when I wake,
God my watch-keep,
God my hope-sake.

God my life-whole,
God lips apart,
God in my soul,
God in my heart.

God Wine and Bread,
God in my death,
God my soul-thread,
God ever breath.

Traditional Gaelic

TEN

A LIVING PILGRIMAGE?

The developing inheritance of the Christian gospel is in itself a living pilgrimage. This pilgrimage owes much to the religious life, and in later centuries particularly to the Benedictine tradition, which has played an essential part in the development of European culture.

The lives of the saints have often been punctuated with uncertainty and suffering; significant numbers of them have ended their lives as martyrs. Even after death their remains have often been the subject of controversy and uncertainty. Thomas Becket's bones were translated from one part of Canterbury Cathedral to another in the year 1220. In 1538 during the reign of Henry VIII they were exhumed and destroyed along with Becket's shrine. Cuthbert was buried on Lindisfarne, but during the ninth-century Danish invasions, his followers exhumed his apparently incorrupt body and moved it around the Border country seeking a safe resting place. They stopped for a time in Norham, in Ripon and at Chester-le-Street. Finally, when the coast was clear, Cuthbert's body reached its final destination in 995, when a great shrine was built for the saint behind the high altar in Durham Cathedral.

The fate of Benedict's remains was different again, but with him too, death would prove to be a continuing pilgrimage. He died in *c.* 547 (some say 560) at the monastery which he founded in Monte Cassino, south of Rome. Monte Cassino was destroyed only a generation later by the Lombards. A late seventeenth-century tradition describes how the abbot of Fleury read the Dialogues of Gregory and was distressed to think that the relics of both Benedict and his sister, Saint Scholastica, lay abandoned in the ruins of Monte Cassino. (The *Dialogues of Gregory the Great* contained the first biography of Benedict.) Scholastica's remains were later taken to Juvigny in Lorraine. Benedict's remains were taken to Fleury on the River Loire which then became a popular pilgrim centre. Visiting the great Romanesque church at St-Benoit-sur-Loire remains an awe-inspiring experience. One may make one's own pilgrimage through the twelfth and thirteenth century nave to the remarkable eleventh-century crypt which contains the modern reliquary with Benedict's remains. The regular round of monastic prayer and plain-chant further adds to the atmosphere.

For a variety of reasons, Benedict as a historical figure does not have the living character which we can discover of say St Jerome or St Augustine of Hippo, both of whom lived still further back within the mists of antiquity. The reason for the inadequacy of our picture of Benedict's personality relates both to the paucity of sources and the fact that Gregory's biography was largely hagiographical and miraculous in nature. None the less, Gregory does provide a skeleton of historical information. It would seem that Benedict was born *c.* 480 in Nursia (modern Norcia) in the province of Umbria in Italy. Benedict went to Rome to study the liberal arts or 'letters' in the equivalent of what later became known as a grammar school. He studied fairly briefly and then opted for the monastic life. He travelled (still accompanied by his nurse) first to Enfide (now Affide) and then, shaking off his nurse, he settled at Subiaco, about fifty miles east of Rome in stunningly wild but beautiful country.

There he lived the life of a solitary in a cave in the hillside for some three years. Benedict's holiness became legendary and he was joined by other disciples. He formed not one large monastery, but twelve small monastic houses each with twelve monks and its own abbot.

Gregory tells us that due to the jealousy of a neighbouring priest Benedict was effectively forced to leave Subiaco, taking a few monks with him, and settling eventually at Monte Cassino. Here he converted the local people from semi-paganism to Christianity, transforming the temple of Apollo into an oratory of St Martin. The pattern Benedict established at Monte Cassino was different from that which he founded in Subiaco. After the fashion of his Rule, he established one large community where the monks were grouped in tens under the leadership of a dean, who was responsible to the abbot. Although Benedict's Rule may not have been composed in one sitting, it is likely that it was written after some experience of Monte Cassino and that it was probably completed in about the year 540. Clearly he was also dependent on at least one prior source, the so-called 'Rule of the Master'.

Benedict's Rule is a masterpiece of balance and of practical wisdom and common sense. It values order and discipline; it is rooted in Holy Scripture; it is characterized by a remarkable lack of rigidity. In its clear description of the structure of the community, and its assumption that abbot and monks will respect each other even though the abbot is the focus of authority, it is a model for Christian relationship – although it should certainly not be mistaken for either democracy or autocracy. The abbot is the spiritual leader, but he will lead by listening, by taking counsel and by seeking the mind of the community. The prologue to the Rule sets the scene from its very first words:

Listen my son to the instructions of your Master, turn the ear
of your heart to the advice of a loving father; accept it will-
ingly and carry it out vigorously; so that through the toil of
obedience you may return to him from whom you have separated by the sloth of disobedience?[1]

Many commentators have emphasized the significance of that
first word, 'Listen'. It is both the foundation of healthy community and the keystone for interpreting Scripture and tradition
within the context of a developing Christian life. It remains the
basis of a living tradition both within the religious life (many
other religious rules are developments of Benedict's) and within European culture more widely. Indeed, in revisiting Benedict
and the sites associated with him we are privileged to encounter a continuous pattern of life in a manner which is impossible with the holy sites of the Celtic tradition. This living
encounter is possible both through the religious communities
which continue to follow Benedict's rule and through the foundations set up in medieval times as Benedictine monasteries
and which continue now as great churches and cathedrals.

In both Iona and Lindisfarne, the inheritance of the Irish
monastic tradition would eventually be succeeded by a Benedictine community on the same site. Jarrow and Wearmouth were
founded by Benedict Biscop who took his name in honour of
the founder of western monasticism. Wilfrid's abbeys at Ripon
and Hexham were both based upon the Benedictine Rule. The
tradition has survived within Anglicanism despite the dissolu-
tion of the monasteries under Henry VIII and the discontinuities
caused by the Reformation. The great abbey churches at Hexham, Sherborne and Tewkesbury and the cathedrals at Canterbury, Durham, Winchester and Norwich are all foundations
that owe their origins to Benedict and his Rule. Four more of
the pre-Reformation cathedrals fall into this same category, and

four monastic foundations established as cathedrals after the Reformation were originally Benedictine houses.

In some of these places, the patterns of monastic life are still easily rediscovered, even though some of the buildings may now be used for rather different purposes. Norwich is a classical example. The great monastic church, with its nave for the worship of the people and its choir where the monks sang the 'hours', retains its role as cathedral of the diocese as it did before the Reformation. The great cloister remains intact, and the ancient library occupies the upper part of the south range of the cloister. The Deanery is the Prior's House and has been the residence of the Priors and then the Deans since the thirteenth century; the medieval Prior's Hall, which is part of the Deanery, is still used to entertain the guests of the cathedral. The cellarers' lodging's are now houses, as are the remains of the great granary and the brewhouse and bakehouse. The Close and the cathedral community still preserve a degree of collegiate life which is part of the Benedictine inheritance. The Anglican tradition of large rectories, capable of offering hospitality, is another aspect of the Benedictine inheritance. Perhaps pre-eminently, the pattern of daily offices, revised by Thomas Cranmer and alluded to in the last chapter also derive directly from Benedict and his Rule.

Alongside this 'modified inheritance' stand, of course, the contemporary Benedictine communities and congregations within both the Roman Catholic and Anglican Churches. To take part in Terce or Vespers at Quarr Abbey on the Isle of Wight or at Glenstal Abbey, near Limerick in the west of Ireland, is to enter again into that same stream of holiness, rooted in the Rule that issued from Benedict's experience at Monte Cassino. The great schools at Ampleforth and Downside, and the university foundation of St Benet's Hall in Oxford, are a contemporary testimony to the scholarly life which was already pioneered in the Celtic monastic tradition, a tradition which flowered throughout Europe in the later Middle Ages. Similarly, within the Anglican tradition, Elmore Abbey is the same community which produced Dom Gregory Dix, perhaps the pioneer of modern liturgical scholarship. At Burford, the double community of women and men is a further testimony to the re-establishment of the religious life in the Church of England. At Burford, the buildings themselves are a fascinating example of the mingling of traditions – the earlier part of the house is the remains of a pre-Reformation Augustinian hospital, whereas the chapel is post-Reformation and was dedicated by the Bishop of Oxford in 1662, the year of publication of the Book of Common Prayer.

LIVING PILGRIMAGE

In the context of a book which seeks to uncover the roots of the Christian faith in these islands in relation particularly to the Celtic and Roman missions, why now focus on Benedict? For it would certainly be mistaken to assume somehow that the shift from the Celtic monastic tradition to Benedictism was simply more of the same. Earlier on we noted the shape of the Celtic monasteries: they were far looser in structure than the later Western pattern and tended (rather after the style of some of the earlier monasteries in the Egyptian desert) to accommodate a number of monks within a monastic enclosure around an oratory. Other significant differences existed, some of which related directly to the differences between the Celtic and Roman traditions which we explored in earlier chapters. The transition, then, was not smooth, although there is some sense of a developing inheritance.

It has become clear throughout this book that the inheritance which gave birth to a renewed Christian mission in the sixth and seventh centuries, particularly in England, was after all a common inheritance. Although there are distinct local characteristics and traditions within Christianity in the seventh century, ultimately roots go back to a common apostolic source. As the two missions advanced towards each other, so there was bound to be interaction and at times conflict. This is usually portrayed classically in the form of a gladiatorial contest at the Synod of Whitby. However, the two traditions grew alongside each other for years to come and there was a gradual but rich cross-fertilization.

The eventual establishment of Benedictine monasteries on Iona and Lindisfarne, and elsewhere at earlier Celtic sites, does mean that the black monks inherited the role in these places earlier vested in the Irish tradition. The powerful part played by Wilfrid also points towards an eventual meeting of the traditions. After his journeys to Rome, Wilfrid would bring back the Benedictine observance. This was the same observance as that of Gregory the Great and Augustine, who were responsible for the Canterbury mission. The Benedictine expansion and flowering throughout the early Middle Ages was arguably the most powerful instrument in the shaping of Europe. It meant effectively, too, that the Christian life became a living pilgrimage; each monastery attempted to mirror the divine life, of the existence of heaven here on earth.

This vision of the Christian life as a living pilgrimage echoes the portrait painted in the first chapter of this book where the image of pilgrimage is applied to the Christian life as a whole. Reference to both holy sites and indeed to missionaries and saints throughout the ages gives to this pilgrim image a clearer focus. Often monasteries became sites of pilgrimage themselves. The great monastic churches gathered in their naves not only local people, but those who came to seek counsel, hospitality, solace or even sanctuary. This had already begun to happen within the Irish and Celtic traditions, where the monasteries became missionary centres. They were minsters which would act as the focus for local Christian people, to some degree in parallel to the Roman tradition of dioceses. The remarkable Benedictine network throughout Europe would later on allow this pattern of living pilgrimage to develop more widely. Anniversaries of the death of saints or of the arrival of missionaries has acted, over the centuries, as a further focus for pilgrimage.

In our present age, where greater insecurity is provoked by the speed of cultural change, it is tempting to allow patterns of pilgrimage to degenerate into nostalgia; the focus becomes entirely historical in a retrospective sense. But part of the radical influence of historical study is its ability to challenge later generations. Clearly the medieval monastic communities orientated themselves sharply towards the future in God. They were 'eschatological' in slant, that is they looked forward to the final consummation of all things when God's kingdom would be established. The great pilgrimage traditions at Compostela, Canterbury, Walsingham or Durham reflected a forward-looking perspective. The same was true of the influence asserted by Armagh, Iona, St Davids or Lindisfarne. The key was a focus upon the future kingdom of God. In that sense there was continuity between the early monasteries of Ireland and Northumbria and the later Benedictines.

BENEDICT AND THE CELTS

Perhaps the most distinctive principle within the Rule of St Benedict is that of stability. This principle aims to anchor the monk in a particular monastery, allowing the individual within community to make an inner spiritual journey or pilgrimage. Wandering ascetics were viewed with much suspicion by Benedict in his Rule:

> The fourth kind of monk are those called Wanderers. These are never stable throughout their whole lives but wanderers through diverse regions receiving hospitality in the monastic cells of others for three or four days at a time, following their own wills, enslaved by the attractions of gluttony.

Here the Irish and Benedictine patterns largely coincided. Steadiness, perseverance and spiritual stability were central to the Irish monasteries. Even the more missionary and peripatetic Celtic monks retained an inner stability alongside their constant journeying.

The community basis for the monastic life is that element within which the Irish and Benedictine traditions probably diverged most profoundly. The more complex liturgical traditions of Benedict's disciples were also at odds with Celtic simplicity. This meant in fact that in Ireland the Cistercians and Augustinian canons were more successful in taking root. Flexibility and enthusiasm for evangelism would have attracted the Irish also to the Augustinian way. The ascetic strain within the Cistercian Rule would have appealed to the Irish inheritance where monasteries had been set in lonely, wild and austere places. In England, too, the Cistercians would choose remote sites; Fountains and Rievaulx are but two examples.

In Northumbria we can see something of the transition from the pure Irish pattern towards Benedictine monasticism. We have seen how the Irish and Roman patterns began to fuse; Whitby was not a Roman triumph but rather initiated the coming together of the two traditions. Cuthbert is perhaps the key transition figure on Lindisfarne. Formed in the Irish rule by

St Boisil at Melrose, Cuthbert remained open to development through the interaction of the two traditions. Cuthbert was clearly a figure who brought order and balance to the life of Lindisfarne through the teaching of a 'rule'. In his *Life of Cuthbert*, Bede writes:

> So when Cuthbert came to the church and monastery of Lindisfarne he handed on the monastic rule by teaching and example; moreover he continued his custom of frequent visits to the common people in the neighbourhood ...

Although it is almost certain that Wilfrid first brought the Rule of St Benedict to Northumbria, it is possible and perhaps even likely that Cuthbert followed soon after. Evidence from Bede's *Life* suggests that Cuthbert almost certainly knew Benedict's Rule and was influenced by it, although it will not have been his sole guide. It is unlikely that he lived under it and was himself a Benedictine.

Even with Wilfrid it is inappropriate simply to call him a Benedictine, although certainly he was more Benedictine in spirit than his contemporaries. It was probably during Wilfrid's second period at his monastery in Ripon that he introduced the Rule of St Benedict. Eddius writes:

> He brought about a great improvement in the church by introducing the Rule of St Benedict. He was another St Paul, opening in these parts the great door of faith.

Although Cuthbert was certainly a better monk than Wilfrid, it was Wilfrid who would be responsible for introducing and nourishing the existence of Benedictine spirituality. The way of Benedict was more balanced and orderly and thus less extreme than the Celtic monastic tradition. Wilfrid began that process in England, which others spread throughout Europe, whereby art, music and architecture were all stimulated and nourished through the Benedictine network of monasteries. Both Cuthbert and Wilfrid in their joint influence anticipated the later and rich diversity of the Benedictine observance.

Hilda, in some ways offers parallels to the influence of Cuthbert. Hilda was not herself strictly a Benedictine and probably never used the Rule. Nevertheless, she helped prepare the development of English monasticism for the later growth of Benedictine life. She stressed the importance of having property in common and of the significance of scripture for the holy life. Both these alongside a stress upon prudence, 'the strict observance of justice, piety, chastity and other virtues, and particularly of peace and charity', suggest strong affinities with Benedict's Rule.

The transition to a preponderance of Benedictine houses was then gradual, and in Northumbria and indeed Wessex there was a most fruitful intermingling of two different traditions. Often a variety of rules stood alongside each other in the same monastery. We saw this at Lindisfarne and Whitby. The richest integration of these different traditions is seen perhaps most markedly in the life of Boniface. Born and educated in Wessex he would lead the apostolic mission in both Holland and Germany. In accepting the missionary road as his vocation he followed the peripatetic path of Columbanus and other early Irish missionaries. The mixture of the spontaneity of the Irish tradition and the organization of the Roman pattern was captured perfectly in Boniface's interpretation of the Benedictine way. Again the potent mixture of art, scholarship and teaching made such Anglo-Saxon monasteries centres of civilization and stability in an often insecure and violent world. It is easy to forget the symbiosis of the mainland European and the British/Irish Christian traditions at this time: Boniface, Willibrord,

Willibald and Wilfrid are just some of those names which exemplify the Europeanism of the gospel even in the early Middle Ages. It was this Europeanism that was to be communicated with great richness as Benedict's disciples took his Rule across Europe and further encouraged the development of education and culture in its widest sense.

THE BUILDING OF EUROPE

To define Europe is to set out on a journey of discovery almost as complex and mysterious as the quest for the Holy Grail. Europe is an elusive concept historically, geographically and culturally. Some would trace it to the reign of Charlemagne while others might delay its emergence until the Renaissance, and the growth of the humanist tradition. However, even in the early mediaeval period, before the advent of a common European culture, there developed an exchange as the result of trade, conflict, and Christian monasticism. Indeed, the growth of the monastic tradition was essential to the building of Europe. From this early period we can trace the more primitive monastic foundations upon which the Benedictine network was founded.

The growth of the Benedictine observance is remarkable. At first this was not so. In Italy it was little known outside Monte Cassino. Indeed, it spread more quickly in France and England than in Italy in the seventh century. The apostolic mission under Augustine and the diligence and energy of Wilfrid were doubtless keys to this expansion. But if Benedict's Rule was slow to gain popularity initially, what was the reason for its eventual growth and indeed dominance within European culture? Almost certainly it was the patronage or even enforcement by the Carolingian dynasty that led to its earliest growth. The Carolingian dynasty saw the order and balance of the Rule as an essential tool for stable secular government. The Carolingian Kings encouraged the foundation and strengthening of Benedictine communities.

Although patronage was essential to establish the rapid and effective spread of Benedictine communities, it was the order and discipline of the Rule itself which made it the obvious candidate to catch the discerning eye of the Carolingian dynasty. It should be added that it would require different forces and circumstances to foster its growth in certain parts of Europe. So, in England, for example, political stability was not really consolidated fully until after the Norman Conquest. Although the Benedictines' influence had already grown by then, it was to grow apace rather later. In 1134 there were thirty Benedictine houses in England; there were three hundred by the turn of the next century. Even a brief glance at an historical map of Britain and Ireland reveals an extraordinary network of monastic foundations. Few of us live far from the ruins or site of an ancient abbey, or from a living church or cathedral founded within that tradition.

It is important to stress that the monasteries did not exist purely for the sake of the monks and for the perfection of their spiritual lives on their pilgrimage to heaven. Richard Southern points to three chief functions for which they existed.[3] He describes these as social, penitential and family functions. The monasteries had a *social* function on behalf of their founders and benefactors inasmuch as they were to conduct a battle against supernatural enemies. It was a battle for the safety of the land and this was closely connected to the battle for the safety of the souls of the benefactors. The *penitential* function allowed monasteries to undertake penance for the great men of the land. Finally, the *family* function allowed noble families to provide for their children by offering them to monasteries; this might well promise them a comfortable and even aristocratic life. This picture outlines the background to the growth and indeed the prosperity of the mediaeval Benedictine foundations. By now, both society as a whole and the religious communities have moved toward a far more structured existence.

Although the tradition of 'trans-European' missionary monks (after the style of Boniface) begins to wither, particularly in the light of the demand for stability, nevertheless this remarkable monastic network became a most effective instrument of the Church's mission, since it was essential to the fabric of medieval European society. It is hard to see how the Carolingian Empire could have prospered without the monasteries as part of the infrastructure. Furthermore, the role of the Benedictine houses educationally was essential to the effective mission of the Church. In all this, the Rule is clear that the recruitment of suitable postulants into the community is an essential.

At the height of their power and influence (in the later middle ages there was a decline) the Benedictine world produced a series of remarkable 'European' scholars and ecclesiastical leaders. Anselm of Aosta, Bec, and later of Canterbury, is perhaps the most outstanding example. The tradition which culminated in Anselm was the richest flowering of a pattern of life whose roots can be traced back well beyond the more advanced structures of Benedictine life. The communities at Kells, on Lindisfarne, at Ripon and Whitby, for example, gathered together an extraordinarily rich variety of influences, both Celtic and Roman in origin. They formed part of a complex and interrelated European civilization, drawing its nourishment in the arts, in scholarship, and in government from the religious life. This life centred on the liturgy which itself was founded upon the gospel of sacrificial love lived and taught by Christ himself.

CELEBRATING LIVING PILGRIMAGE

It was Pope Paul VI who declared Benedict to be the Patron of Europe. In our present age we are frequently bidden to reflect upon the European and indeed universal nature of our faith. In the mid-twentieth century, the experience of two World Wars stimulated Jean Monnet and Robert Schuman to work for a new European vision. It was a vision that deliberately began with concrete economic aims; its origins lay in the European Coal and Steel Community. Underpinning these economic aims was a more profound vision rooted in the historic Christian culture stemming from Carolingian times and nourished by the monastic communities. Schuman and Monnet, and indeed more recently Jacques Delors, have been inspired by their Christian faith to rekindle a sense of the 'soul of Europe'. Historical reflection from within the community of faith provoked a sense of responsibility for the whole of Europe.

In recent years this pan-European vision has been echoed, too, in specifically religious contexts: The Papal Youth Pilgrimages, the European Ecumenical Gathering at Basel in 1989 (sponsored by all the Churches of Europe – Catholic, Orthodox, Anglican and Protestant) and the annual Taizé Young People's Pilgrimages held in different European capitals after Christmas every year. Each of these in its own way is a celebration of living pilgrimage, and indeed each of them points beyond to the wider implications of Christianity for the life of humanity. Ecology, social justice, peace and the development of human community, and respect for life, form the agendas for all these gatherings.

Within Britain and Ireland, more modest gatherings of young people particularly celebrate the living pilgrimage which is Christianity. Even the annual youth festivals – Greenbelt and Spring Harvest (and numerous others) – are different manifestations of this same phenomenon. It is important to hold together both the pan-European and the national/local celebrations, for this reflects so much of what we have discovered in these past ten chapters. It reflects, too, the preoccupations which have stood at the heart of the debate about Europe in the past few years. It is not a case of either the European or the national, either the universal or the local. Both aspects lie central to our humanity and to our faith. Our Irishness, Welshness, Scottishness or Englishness are to be celebrated and cherished but they are to be offered to the wider community of nations. Our European inheritance is again the cause for celebration, but it should be the basis neither of the 'European standard eucharist' nor of a fortress perspective towards the wider international community. Europe, just like individual nation states, has something to offer to the rest of the human community, and it also has much to receive. Equally, Europe is not there to standardize, inhibit or crush the individual gifts of nations or indeed churches.

The celebrations of 1997 are a gift which can only be received and celebrated once in every hundred years. The gift is particularly precious since it is a potent reminder of the common faith which we all share. Gregory and Augustine, Columba and Aidan, Ciaran, Patrick, David, Piran, Ninian, Wilfrid and the galaxy of early saints who brought the gospel to these islands all preached the same gospel of salvation offered to humanity by God, through our Lord Jesus Christ. But this common faith is one which is offered in the richest variety of different patterns and colours. After centuries of neglect, we have begun once again to treasure the individuality and richness of the Celtic tradition. In it we find strands which resonate with themes which have surfaced in the contemporary world, albeit in different guises – the integrity of the created universe, the place of women within society, the significance of contemplative prayer. None of these themes is absent in other manifestations of Christianity, but the Celtic monks expressed these themes uniquely; they were shaped by the landscape within which they grew.

This rediscovery has profound lessons to teach us about all traditions. In each there is a unique, individual expression of the gospel message which feeds into a richer whole. One of the remarkable facets of the Benedictine spirit is the way it embraces both a universality and allows sufficient space for each member of the community to offer her/his own contribution. Pilgrimage also brings together the individual and the community. Chaucer's pilgrims were all individual characters – sometimes rumbustious, sometimes holy and sometimes profoundly unattractive. But on pilgrimage they shared a common destination and journey. Pilgrimage is an image which is powerful for us at any time in our own journey and in the journey of the people of God – we are the Church, we are the body of Christ, we are always on the way, *in via*, we are ... pilgrims.

Prayer

Today we are far from home
And have lost the key to the door.
But you call us to go in
And find ourselves again.
Your invitation is to the interior life,
Your experience is that of persons
Who regain a sense of themselves.
Benedict teach us the way back to the heart,
In Christ our Lord. Amen.

Prayer on the shrine of St Benedict at Fleury, St-Benoit-sur-Loire.

Gracious and holy Father, give us wisdom to perceive you, diligence to seek you, patience to wait for you, eyes to behold you; a heart to meditate on you, and a life to proclaim you; through the power of the Spirit of Jesus Christ our Lord. Amen.

St Benedict

NOTES ON SOURCES

CHAPTER ONE

1 Bruce Chatwin, 'Dreaming', *Granta* 21 (1987): 45;79.
2 Quoted in Henry Mayr-Harting, *The Coming of Christianity to Anglo-Saxon England*, 3rd edition, London, 1991.
3 Kenneth Kirk, *The Vision of God*, Cambridge, 1977.

CHAPTER THREE

1 'Boswell's Journal of a Tour to the Hebrides', from the collected *Boswell's Life of Johnson*, vol. 5. Oxford, 1964, p. 334.
2 Anton Wessels, *Europe: Was it Ever Really Christian?* London, 1994, pp. 72–3, quoting O'Cathasaigh, 'A Study of Pagan Christian Syncretism'.
3 Anthony Duncan, *The Elements of Celtic Christianity*, Shaftesbury, 1992, p.134.

CHAPTER FOUR

1 Mayr-Harting, p. 135.
2 G. W. O. Addleshaw, *The Beginnings of the Parochial System*, London, 1953, p. 7.
3 R. W. Southern, *The Making of the Middle Ages*, London, 1953 (repr. 1993), p. 73.

CHAPTER FIVE

1 Cf. 'St Hilda and St Etheldreda', by Dame Etheldreda Hession in *Benedict's Disciples*, ed. David Hugh Farmer, Leominster, 1980, pp. 70–85.
2 Mayr-Harting, p. 129.
3 Christopher Dawson, *Understanding Europe*, London, 1952, pp. 31 ff.
4 Cf. R. W. Southern, *Saint Anselm: A Portrait in a Landscape*, Cambridge, 1990, pp. 308 ff.

CHAPTER SIX

1 *Faith in the City*, London, 1985, p. xv.
2 Cf. Jean-Marie Tillard, *L'Église des Églises*, translated as *Church of Churches: The Ecclesiology of Communion*, Collegeville, 1992, and John Zizioulas, *Being as Communion*, New York, 1985.
3 WCC, *Baptism, Eucharist and Ministry*, Geneva, 1982.
4 Anglican-Roman Catholic International Commission, *The Final Report*, London, 1982, pp. 57–8.
5 James D. G. Dunn, *Unity and Diversity in the New Testament*, London, 1977, p. 32.
6 Vincent Donovan, *Christianity Rediscovered*, London, 1982, pp. 80, 189.

CHAPTER SEVEN

1 For evidence of a similar apporach to implicit religion within Paul's own writings see Romans 2:14–16.
2 Cf. particularly the works of Karl Barth and the rise of so-called Neo-Orthodoxy. Both stressed the revelation of God and the redemption wrought in Jesus Christ.
3 Karl Barth's Neo-Orthodoxy denied the possibility of natural theology; humanity must be confronted by God's self-revelation. Some extreme biblical critics have effectively denied the power of the Holy Scriptures to reveal God to humanity.
4 Nora Chadwick, *The Age of the Saints in the Early Celtic Church*, London, 1961, p. 83.
5 Wesley Carr, *Brief Encounters*, London 1985, p. 42.

CHAPTER EIGHT

1 Kenneth Jackson in *Studies in the Early British Church*, Cambridge, 1958, p. 311.
2 Quoted by Esther de Waal, *The Celtic Vision*, London, 1988, p. 26.
3 Quoted in Esther de Waal, *A World Made Whole*, London, 1991, p. 67. (A new edition of this book, under the title *Celtic Light*, is to be published by Fount Paperbacks early in 1997.)
4 *A World Made Whole*, p. 129.

CHAPTER NINE

1 Quoted from the *Carmina Gadelica* by Esther de Waal in *The Celtic Vision*, p. 8.
2 Martin Reith, *God in our Midst*, London, 1975, p. 26.
3 See, for example, the prayers of David Adam in *The Edge of Glory*, London, 1985; *Tides and Seasons*, London, 1989.

Notes on Sources

4 Martin Reith, *God in our Midst*, pp. 20, 22.
5 Kenneth Kirk, *The Vision of God*, London, 1932, pp. 101, 465. For a more accessible version, closer to the original Bampton Lectures, see Kenneth Kirk, *The Vision of God*, Abridged Edition, Cambridge, 1977.

CHAPTER TEN
1 This translation from David Parry, *Households of God*, London, 1980, p. 1.

QUESTIONS FOR
DISCUSSION ON FIVE THEMES

THE LOCAL AND THE UNIVERSAL (CHAPTERS 1 AND 6)
1 How does your church community benefit from membership of the wider Church?
2 What local issues or circumstances have influenced the life of the Christian community in your area?
3 How can thinking of life as a pilgrimage help us as individuals, and as a community?
4 How are we to cherish our national and local heritage at the same time as embracing the common humanity of which everyone is a part?.

PILGRIMAGE AND MISSION (CHAPTERS 2 AND 7)
1 Would you be prepared to accept the conversion of a temple of another faith into a Christian church or the conversion of a redundant church into a place of worship for another faith? Why?
2 'The truth is that we are mongrels' (page 43). Are we the better for it?
3 How do the Church boundaries and regulations help and/or hinder the work of mission?
4 Having discovered God's mission ourselves, how do we make a godless world recognize that God is already present?

CREATION AND WHOLENESS (CHAPTERS 3 AND 8)
1 How can the Celtic concept of the integrity of creation enrich our worship and our lives?
2 What can the medical world and the Church learn from the Celtic approach to healing?
3 Which local or national groups in your experience fall into the trap of being 'issue-based' (page 163)? How do others avoid it?

PRAYER AND ACTION (CHAPTERS 4 AND 9)

1 What were the attractions of the Christian religion that led hundreds to be baptized in the River Glen in Northumbria, or were they just following their lords and masters?

2 'The presence of personalities like that of Wilfrid made the Synod of Whitby a necessity.' What was there in Wilfrid's personality that made the Synod necessary?

3 Is it true that modern life has become alienated from the natural world by life in cities? Cannot life in cities actually enhance our awareness of the natural world when we leave the city?

4 Unceasing prayer: is it possible?

LIVING TRADITION (CHAPTERS 5 AND 10)

1 Look dispassionately at life in your local church. Do you feel yourself to be an inheritor of the Roman or Celtic tradition? Are you happy with this, and if not, in which direction would you wish to move, and why?

2 What do you see as the key distinguishing features of the Roman and Celtic traditions?

3 Which of the saints discussed in this book have the most to teach us about the Christian journey today?

FURTHER READING

PRIMARY SOURCES
Ecclesiastical History of the English People, The Venerable Bede, Revised Edition, Harmondsworth, 1990.
The Age of Bede, Harmondsworth, 1988.

GENERAL
The Coming of Christianity to Anglo-Saxon England, Henry Mayr-Harting, 3rd edition, London, 1991.
The Making of the Middle Ages, R. W. Southern, London, 1953 (repr. 1993).
Western Society and the Church in the Middle Ages, R. W. Southern, Harmondsworth, 1970.
Europe: Was it Ever Really Christian? Anton Wessels, London, 1994.

CELTIC BACKGROUND
The Elements of Celtic Christianity, Anthony Duncan, Shaftesbury, 1992.
God in our Midst, Martin Reith, London, 1975.
Living Between Worlds, Philip Sheldrake, London, 1995.
Celtic Journeys in Scotland and the North of England, Shirley Toulson, Fount Paperbacks, London, 1996.
The Celtic Vision, Esther de Waal, London, 1988.
A World Made Whole, Esther de Waal, London, 1991. (A new edition of this book, under the title *Celtic Light*, is to be published by Fount Paperbacks, London, early in 1997.)

ST BENEDICT
Households of God, David Parry (The Rule with Commentary), London, 1980.
Seeking God, Esther de Waal, Revised Edition, Fount Paperbacks, London, 1996.